CLIMATE E/

SocietyNow

SocietyNow: short, informed books, explaining why our world is the way it is, now.

The SocietyNow series provides readers with a definitive snapshot of the events, phenomena and issues that are defining our 21st century world. Written leading experts in their fields, and publishing as each subject is being contemplated across the globe, titles in the series offer a thoughtful, concise and rapid response to the major political and economic events and social and cultural trends of our time.

SocietyNow makes the best of academic expertise accessible to a wider audience, to help readers untangle the complexities of each topic and make sense of our world the way it is, now.

Poverty in Britain: Causes, Consequences and Myths
Tracy Shildrick

The Trump Phenomenon: How the Politics of Populism Won in 2016
Peter Kivisto

Becoming Digital: Towards a Post-Internet Society
Vincent Mosco

Understanding Brexit: Why Britain Voted to Leave the European Union
Graham Taylor

Selfies: Why We Love (and Hate) Them
Katrin Tiidenberg

Internet Celebrity: Understanding Fame Online
Crystal Abidin

Corbynism: A Critical Approach
Matt Bolton

The Smart City in a Digital World
Vincent Mosco

Kardashian Kulture: How Celebrities Changed Life in the 21st Century
Ellis Cashmore

Reality Television: The TV Phenomenon that Changed the World
Ruth A. Deller

Drones: The Brilliant, The Bad, and the Beautiful
Andy Miah

Digital Detox: The Politics of Disconnecting
Trine Syvertsen

The Olympic Games: A Critical Approach
Helen Jefferson Lenskyj

Sex and Social Media
Katrin Tiidenberg and Emily van der Nagel

The Politicization of Mumsnet
Sarah Pedersen

Tattoos and Popular Culture
Lee Barron

Disability and Other Human Questions
Dan Goodley

Mark Harvey applies a wide-angle lens to the ultimate global crisis – climate change – demonstrating that a social scientific understanding of the historical development of societal ecologies is crucial. An original contribution of importance to all concerned with understanding problems and solutions.

–Alan Warde, Sustainable Consumption Institute, University of Manchester, UK

Working with and building upon the generative insights of Karl Polanyi, Mark Harvey delivers a penetrating and original analysis of the climate emergency, grounded in an integrative, historical, and comparative method. *Climate Emergency* establishes a new benchmark, and provides new tools, for the critical social-scientific study of global climate change.

–Jamie Peck, University of British Columbia, Canada

Coping with anthropogenic climate change requires us all to "follow the science". This must include the insights of historical and social sciences, which are epiphenomena of the planetary degradation of recent centuries. Mark Harvey's concept of sociogenesis is a landmark contribution, which he operationalizes in this book to explicate the emergency we now face. He highlights the economic and ethical dilemmas not of humanity in the abstract, but of concrete political societies around the world with very unequal endowments and histories.

–Chris Hann, Max Planck Institute for Social Anthropology, Germany

CLIMATE EMERGENCY

How Societies Create the Crisis

BY

MARK HARVEY
University of Essex, UK

United Kingdom – North America – Japan – India
Malaysia – China

Emerald Publishing Limited
Howard House, Wagon Lane, Bingley BD16 1WA, UK

First edition 2021

Reprints and permissions service
Contact: permissions@emeraldinsight.com

British Library Cataloguing in Publication Data
A catalogue record for this book is available from the British Library

ISBN: 978-1-80043-333-5 (Print)
ISBN: 978-1-80043-330-4 (Online)
ISBN: 978-1-80043-332-8 (Epub)

ISOQAR certified
Management System,
awarded to Emerald
for adherence to
Environmental
standard
ISO 14001:2004.

Certificate Number 1985
ISO 14001

INVESTOR IN PEOPLE

CONTENTS

LIST OF FIGURES

ABOUT THE AUTHOR

Mark Harvey is Emeritus Professor at the Sociology Department University of Essex. He was Research Professor from September 2007 to 2019, and established the Centre for Research in Economic Sociology and Innovation. For the previous decade he had been at the ESRC Centre for Research in Innovation and Competition (CRIC) at the University of Manchester, and is now Honorary Professor there in the Sustainable Consumption Institute. With a first degree in History from Oxford, followed by a PhD in Sociology (on Historico-critical Epistemology) from London School of Economics, he held a post-doctoral research fellowship at the Institute of Genetic Epistemology, working with Jean Piaget at the University of Geneva (1968–1970). He was a Lecturer in Sociology and Psychology at Brunel University (1971–1974) before leaving academia to become a building labourer, returning to academia 17 years later in 1993. He was made a honorary life member of the building trades union, UCATT, in 2002 for services to the labour movement.

1

CLIMATE EMERGENCY

Climate change has become a climate emergency. A long history of the human impact on the earth's climate has met with global and national political failure. Following the 2015 Paris Agreement, awareness of the rapidity and extent of climate change and the need to keep warming below 1.5°C called for much more drastic national and international political action to be taken. Instead, there has been stalemate and prevarication, before and especially since the election of climate change denying presidents of the United States and Brazil (Trump and Bolsonaro).

Now, from December 2019, the world has been hit by a very different kind of emergency, the COVID-19 pandemic. In general, the contrast in political responses to the two emergencies could scarcely be greater. The grounding of most of the world's airplane fleets, ironically immediately and sharply reducing CO_2 emissions, was a reaction to the immediate, rather than long-term, threat of hundreds of millions of deaths worldwide. Lockdowns across the world have drastically reduced vehicle traffic on roads, plunging the demand for oil, when only weeks before Russia and OPEC were fighting the

United States for market share in a price war. Another significant reduction in CO_2 emissions, and sharp reduction in air pollution from nitrous oxygen in many of the world's major cities, ensued as an unintended consequence. The International Energy Authority estimates that there has been a 25% drop in total energy demand in lockdown countries, by far the biggest drop in 70 years (IEA, 2020). One might ask whether we need the threat of an immediate culling of the world population to stimulate a politics adequate to deal with the climate emergency.

This contemporary confluence between climate change and a pandemic prompts a reflection on a historical parallel, if one of a much greater scale: the Black Death and the Little Ice Age. Although by no means scientifically consensual, the reduction of human activity arising from a loss of between a quarter and a third of the global human population resulted in abandonment of land, reforestation and the reduction of methane emissions from livestock (Ruddiman, 2010).[1] The resultant if time-lagged cooling of the planet then produced a vicious cycle of crop failures and famines. In turn, apart from the major economic and social consequences of the scarcity of labour, the economic collapse had a dramatic impact on the finances of European (and other) states. It has been argued that the plague-induced financial crises of states in Europe, China, India and Africa lay behind decades of political turbulence and national and civil wars (Parker, 2013). And, finally, in a dark resonance with the present, there were the historical equivalents of lockdowns, with plague banishments and forced isolations.

The significance for climate change of these two pandemics, differing in scale and hopefully duration, is that they

---

1 'Plague-driven CO2 decreases were probably most important just after 1350 AD and between 1500 AD and 1750 AD' (Ruddiman, 2003, p. 290).

dramatically reduced human activity, either by political fiat as in today's case, or by the relentless and recurrent depopulation of the earlier period. While the advance of scientific knowledge might solve the immediate biological threats by means of vaccines and therapies, the political capacities to resolve the resultant economic crisis are deeply uncertain. Likewise, for the climate emergency, in spite of the overwhelming scientific understanding of the effects of particular kinds of greenhouse gas emitting human activity, steps to reduce or replace that activity have proved substantially inadequate. It is clear that, unlike curing a disease, there is no straightforward technical fix.

A central argument of this book is that in important ways there has been a failure to diagnose the complex and varied nature of the climate emergency. Or rather, there have been enormous advances in the natural scientific understanding of the climate change, and a relatively laggardly development of social scientific and historical understanding of what has been and is a complex, multiple and varied combination of historical societal processes. As we shall shortly see, environmental sciences have rightly focused on physical processes of burning fossil fuels, deforestation and land-use change, and their effects on the planet's atmosphere, inducing global warming. To understand the physical processes, in a sense it doesn't matter who is doing it and why. It is reasonable for natural sciences to bracket off the who and why, and just observe and analyse the physical effects as a consequence of human activity in general. Hence, within these disciplines it is quite justifiable to speak of 'anthropogenic' climate change, climate change induced by 'the human', the no-matter-what human. The crucial insight that a new geological period has been entered when a unique species has, for the first time, had the capacity to fundamentally alter the earth's atmosphere dictates their choice of a name: the Anthropocene. There is, natural scientifically speaking, no problem with these terms. But they cannot be imported into a social scientific account of the climate emergency, which needs to complement, rather than contest, the conceptual and empirical work of natural science with that of social science.

The who, the how and the why are the central questions for any social scientific understanding of climate change in the first place, and then the why it has become the climate emergency. So the perspective advocated here adopts the term 'sociogenic' to embrace the complex dynamics of how societies make the climate change crisis. Likewise, rather than adopting a geological time-frame of 'the anthropocene' – and we will see that there are debates amongst environmental scientists as to when that began – an historical and comparative social science approach needs to delineate historical phases and different historical societal trajectories accelerating and modifying the physical processes of climate change.

One of the key arguments of the book therefore grasps what has been called 'the great divergence' as a key period of history affecting climate change (Pomeranz, 2000). It was the time when Northern Europe both began to industrialise and to expand and colonise the New World, relying on the development of mass plantation slavery (Harvey, 2019). This political, social and economic transformation both accelerated climate change and created new levels of inequality, both between and within societies across the globe. Northern Europe diverged from China, India, Japan and other societies which had been roughly equal in prosperity before then. Inequality and climate change are coeval, an entanglement which, as we shall see, is central to any social scientific analysis of climate change and to the political obstacles to overcoming it.

Before setting on this road to social scientific understanding, and developing the concept of sociogenesis, it is

worth recognising fully where natural science has now got us
in understanding the climate emergency. In 2000, the term
Anthropocene was coined, recognising fully for the first time
that human beings were the one species capable of altering
the planet's atmosphere (Crutzen, 2002; Crutzen &
Stoermer, 2000). At the time, it was suggested that the
new geological epoch, 'supplementing the Holocene', began
in the latter part of the eighteenth century. Indeed, the culprit
was identified and named: James Watt, designer of the coal-
fired steam engine, icon of the British industrial revolution.
However, even in these early papers, the 'expansion of
mankind' was predicated on the expansion of agriculture.
Conversion of 'wild' nature into cultivated nature through
domestication of plants and animals released CO_2 and the
much more powerful greenhouse gas, methane, and was
seen as a major source of climate change. Indeed, even
those papers that advocate the eighteenth century as the
commencement date for the Anthropocene allude to the fact
that while the human population increased by 10-fold over
three centuries, the number of cattle emitting methane grew
at a much faster pace. By the time the global population had
reached six billion the number of domesticated cattle reached
14 billion.

Imagine a planet without the transformational activity of
humans. All things being equal, the earth is subject to regular
periods of glaciation followed by warming during the interglacial period, reaching a peak, before atmospheric temperatures
decline towards the next glaciation. The current interglacial
period, the Holocene, was already turning on a downwards
cooling pathway. Without setting a formal date for the
commencement of the Anthropocene, those arguing for an
alternative perspective for initiating anthropogenic climate
change point to the atypical presence of CO_2 and methane
(CH_4) in ice cores at levels that can only be plausibly accounted

for by human activity. Widespread deforestation with the
spread of agriculturalist human societies, the domestication and
cultivation of rice in China 5,000 years ago, and the domestication and rearing of livestock, it is argued, resulted in planet-
warming if slow changes to earth's atmosphere, countering
expected regular cooling leading towards glaciation. Nearly
40% of the land under rice cultivation today was already in
cultivation a 1000 years ago; and the area of land dedicated to
raising livestock nearly tripled between 3000BC and 1000BC
(Fuller, 2010; Fuller et al., 2011). We will call this the Long
View, as propounded by Ruddiman, Fuller and others, as
distinct from the Industrialisation View.

Although scientists may argue between the Long View and
the Industrialisation View of anthropogenic climate change,
none dispute the rapid acceleration occurring from the end of
the eighteenth century onwards. It was a change of pace
beyond compare, historically speaking. However, the importance attributed to domestication of plants and livestock
advocated by the Long View provides a significant counter-
balance to regarding the rapid acceleration of the later period
as a consequence of industrialisation with the totemic coal-fired
steam engine. The Pomeranz thesis points to the colonisation of
the New World, which, together with the expansion of agricultural land in Eastern Europe, resulted in an exponential
increase in deforestation and land-use change for agriculture. In
different ways in different societies, industrialisation and
urbanisation only developed in combination with agricultural
expansion and intensification. Industrialisation and land-use
change are dynamically related, so it is mistaken to consider
either one or the other as responsible for the rapid acceleration
from the late eighteenth century. Overall, between 1700 and
1890, the area brought under cultivation increased 466%,
again, historically speaking, a rate of change beyond compare.

The figure for North America, given the minimal spread of agriculturalism there before colonisation, was a statistically extreme increase of 6,666% (Meyer & Turner, 1992). Yet this fanciful figure masks a crucial societal and climate change event, discussed further below (Chapter 3): the genocidal replacement of hunter-gatherer Native Americans by the white colonists of slave cotton production and cattle ranching. The first and gradual emergence of agriculturalism displacing hunter-gatherer societies contrasts with the brutal rapidity and scale of change in nineteenth century North America. To date, there has been no natural scientific estimation or modelling of the relative significance of the industrial burning of coal and agricultural expansion between 1750 and 1850, but as one depended on the other, it is only their combination that matters when natural scientists observe the aggregate impact on the Earth System.

Given the fundamental differences between the temporalities of geological interglacial cycles and the irregularities, disruptions and variable temporal and spatial scales of human societal histories, in the end it does not make sense to fix a start date for when human activity initiated a shift into a new geological epoch: the Anthropocene. Geological time and historical time operate on radically different temporalities. It is enough to know that, unless a pandemic eliminates the human species, the physical impacts of human activity on the Earth System are climate changing. The Anthropocene could never have the same kind of beginnings or endings as the Miocene, the Pliocene or the Pleistocene. It is clear – again from within a natural science perspective – that anthropogenic impacts on the earth's planetary system go a very long way back, and that there have been periods of acceleration and deceleration over the millennia.

Setting aside when all this began, therefore, this is how leading earth scientists construct the boundary between environmental and social science:

> *While recognising that different societies around the world have contributed differently and unequally to pressures on the Earth System and will have varied capacities to alter future trajectories,* the sum total of human impacts *(my emphasis) needs to be taken into account for analysing future trajectories of the Earth System.*
>
> (Steffen et al., 2018, p. 8252)

Environmental scientists and cosmologists measure gases in ice-cores, sea temperature and levels, satellite maps of shrinking polar ice cover and mountain glaciers, land-use change and deforestation, and other physical indicators in order to model the effects on the Earth System, conceived of as a physical system. In this way, as the quotation indicates, they bracket off the socioeconomic processes, even societal differences, which generate greenhouse gases only to consider the aggregate total impact of all human activity. They do what social scientists do not and cannot do, leaving the challenge for social science to analyse the historical social/societal processes. There is a division of labour implied in the concepts of 'anthropogenic' and the Anthropocene, not a denial of the significance of historical social/societal processes.

Similarly, pointing a finger at James Watt's steam engine burning coal might be seen as defending a kind of technological determinism of climate change. But, as we shall see there are very different technological trajectories in different societies (Chapters 3, 4, 5). Major new technologies, such as oil as a fossil fuel for terrestrial and air transport or the electrification of domestic and industrial equipment (Chapter 5), or nitrogen phosphate fertilizers all combine to produce an accelerating aggregate impact, but have been developed and adopted in different ways, at different times, in different societies. Nitrogen phosphate fertilizers are a classic instance of the political and social shaping of technological development and adoption. It has been argued that without the invention and adoption of chemical fertilizers the world's population could not have grown from 1.6 billion in 1900 to over six billion by 2000 (Smil, 2004). For 70 years prior to this, European agriculture had increasingly relied on guano and mined nitrates from Peru and Chile. After Britain had encouraged war between Peru and Chile, it gained a 70% control of exports, threatening German production of food. By 1914, nearly 2.5 million tonnes were being imported, mostly to Britain (Clark & Foster, 2009; Melillo, 2012). Consequently, pressure to escape from this British stranglehold stimulated two German scientists (Haber and Bosch) to develop a way of fixing nitrates from the atmosphere, leading to the revolutionary development and use of chemical fertilizers. Already at its birth, nitrogen phosphate fertilizer was therefore a profoundly geopolitical event, not just a technological or physical process event. And it remained so. The politics of food self-sufficiency in China in the contemporary period created an ecological and climate change crisis through overproduction and overuse of chemical fertilizers in rice production (Chapter 4). Nitrogen phosphate was from its birth to its current use in China, a further major source of global warming, quite apart from its significance in enabling urbanisation and industrialisation in different societal contexts. It was equally a physical process, produced by a technology releasing nitrogen oxide into the atmosphere, as analysed by climate scientists (anthropogenic); and a sociopolitical process (sociogenic).

A further natural science concept of great importance is that of 'planetary boundaries' (Rockström et al., 2009; Steffen

et al., 2015), which sets out a range of thresholds and
boundaries for the exploitation of earth's resources beyond
which human sustainability is threatened. It aims to define 'the
safe operating space for humanity'. As with the complementary concepts of the Anthropocene and anthropogenic climate
change, the unit of analysis is The Planet, the total earth
system and aggregate human impacts on it. The concept
broadens the understanding of the nature of the Earth System
crisis by proposing nine different planetary boundaries, of
which climate change and biosphere integrity (broadly preventing a catastrophic loss of biodiversity) are core. Land
system change (deforestation and loss of carbon sinks);
freshwater use (unsustainable levels of ground and surface
water extraction); ocean acidification (as an effect of seawater
temperature rises); atmospheric aerosol loading (especially
urban and industrial particle pollution, notably affecting
weather systems such as monsoons); stratospheric ozone
depletion (as exemplified by the now regulated use of CfCs in
refrigeration); novel entities (the least defined boundary, but
highlighting a risk of novel chemicals or biological entities
threatening human and other species life); and finally
biochemical flows (in particular flows of nitrogen and phos-
phates from chemical fertilizers). As with the concept of the
Anthropocene, the idea of planetary boundaries and the 'safe
operating space for humanity' is framed in terms of achieving
a stability of the interglacial Holocene geological epoch. In
other words, it is setting limits to the impact of the Anthropocene on the Holocene, aspiring to revert to the safety of
geological time.

In developing the concept of planetary boundaries, the
multi-disciplinary group of scientists have emphasised that
there are first thresholds which, if crossed, say at a level
emissions of CO_2 or a scale of deforestation, would lead to a
zone of high and uncertain risk, but a zone which still allowed

for policy steps to be taken to revert to the safe zone. An historical example of banning CfCs in refrigerators to help restore the hole in the ozone would be an example of going beyond a threshold but not irreversibly transgressing a boundary. Another example would be the UK banning the use of coal for urban domestic heating, so reducing aerosol loading, eliminating notorious city smogs. Not so, in today's Delhi or Beijing, or even parts of central London from diesel fumes.

In their analysis of empirical data concerning the planetary boundaries, determining the current state of the Earth System, it is striking that there is high certainty in their judgement about climate change especially from CO_2 emissions. The Earth System is still within the threshold of reversibility, as it is with land-use change (deforestation), oceanic acidification and ozone depletion, but with uncertainties about atmospheric aerosol loading (except those affecting monsoons), and novel physical or biological entities. However, it is equally striking that biochemical flows especially from agricultural fertilizers has gone beyond the boundary into the zone of high risk, as has the rate of species extinctions and loss of biosphere integrity. The modelling of the state of risk in each of the planetary boundary dimensions has been sophisticated further by showing where and how widespread geographically are the locations generating a high risk. In planetary boundary terms, these are the red danger zones. For industrialised agriculture, SE Asia, northern India, northern Europe and north-central USA are highlighted as the hotspots of planetary boundary transgression. From within a natural science optic, these are described as purely physical spatial locations, not political, economic or social units of analysis. The determination of the nature and location of transgressions of planetary boundaries is firmly within the broader conception of the Earth System as a physical, biological and chemical entity. That is what

natural scientists do, and yet, as we shall see hotspots are
socially and politically generated.

As a system, moreover, the nine planetary boundaries refer
not to separate and independent sources of risk to Holocene
stability, but interactive dimensions of a unique planetary
system.[2] There are negative feedback loops arising from
excesses in each of the areas of human impact. Although the
science of these complex systems interactions is at an early
stage, examples of negative feedbacks by which increasing risk
in one dimension creates impacts in another, so causing a
vicious downward spiral are more than speculative doomsday
scenarios. Deforestation of the Amazon can result in a change
in heat convection from the sun and reduction of precipitation
rainfall through areal river streams. In turn, this loss of convection can result in changes in the jet stream which then affects
surface temperature and precipitation in Tibet, leading to a
melting of glaciers thousands of miles away. Another example
of an interaction is to be expected in the melting of the
Greenland Ice Cap resulting in a shift in the Atlantic Meridi-
onal Ocean Circulation, intensifying the warming of the
Southern Ocean, and provoking a more rapid rise in sea-levels.
A very different example is the effect of global warming forcing
an evolution of agricultural animal pests and infections in
Africa, already affecting livestock and further threatening
insecure food supplies (IPCC, 2019). Permafrost thawing is
amongst the highest risk examples of such interactions, provoking a tipping point of accelerated global warming by the
massive release of CO_2 and methane into the atmosphere. On
20 June 2020, the temperature in Verkhoyansk, a town in the
Siberian Arctic Circle, reached a record 38C compared with the

2 'The planetary boundaries framework arises from the scientific evidence that
  Earth is a single, complex, integrated system – that is, the boundaries
  operate as an interdependent set' (Steffen et al., 2015, p. 785).

historic average of 13C. Permafrost has begun to thaw there, leading to collapsing foundations of industrial buildings and roads, aside from releasing methane so creating a feedback loop to climate change. The tipping point is here and now. In turn, one tipping point can trigger another, leading to 'tipping cascades'. It should be clear that these are not yet predictions invested with scientific certainty. But that is perhaps the most important point: risks are being generated without any certainty that they can be contained. The Earth System could tip from a more or less stable system into Hothouse Earth (Steffen et al., 2018), before we had the developed knowledge to understand exactly how and why it was happening. There is, after all, already the strongest evidence that science lagged nearly 200 years behind the great acceleration of the late 18th and early nineteenth century climate change. We are only improving scientific understanding post facto. In short, the risk is that there will only be scientific understanding of what is happening to the Earth System *too late* to do anything about it.

WHEN A CLIMATE CHANGE CRISIS BECOMES A CLIMATE CHANGE EMERGENCY

So too, the climate emergency has only become understood as a climate emergency after it has become an emergency. In 1992, a collective letter from the Union of Concerned Scientists, signed by 1,575 scientists including 99 of the 196 living Nobel laureates, was entitled 'World Scientists' Warning to Humanity'. On the 25th anniversary of that letter, another letter, with the same title was signed by 15,364 scientists from 184 countries, issuing of 'A Second Notice' of warning (Ripple et al., 2018). A year later, a letter, signed by a similar number of scientists from across the globe, was published with a revised and more alarming title: 'World Scientists' Warning of a Climate

Emergency'. The emergency had been named. Between the first letter and the most recent ones, a remarkable transformation of scientific world view has occurred. In the first letter, a wide ranging assessment of 'ever-increasing environmental degradation' was powerfully broadcast. It highlighted and measured the increasing and extensive human damage to the atmosphere, water resources, land, oceans, forests and species variety. The warning ended with an appeal for a great change 'if vast human misery is to be avoided and our global home on this planet is not to be irretrievably mutilated'. But there was no mention of climate change. No mention of CO_2 emissions. No mention of sea level rises or ice-sheet reductions. No mention of burning fossil fuels, or of atmospheric pollution from NOx emissions. No mention of the meat transition and the exponential increase in ruminant livestock.

To be sure, the International Panel on Climate Change had already been established in 1988, and even before that the First World Climate Change Conference had been held in Geneva (1979). The Kyoto Protocol was the first international agreement on climate change mitigation (1997), and by far the most comprehensive treaty agreement was achieved in Paris with COP21 in 2015. Nonetheless, and despite an ever increasing depth and scope of understanding of the climate crisis manifest in multiple IPCC Reports over the years, the climate crisis has been transformed into an emergency.

Although lamenting the weaknesses and failures of successive international conferences under the auspices of the UN, the climate emergency has been defined by natural scientists, as their self-declared moral obligation and necessary contribution to humanity. They portray it as an Earth System emergency. Not as a political or societal emergency. The consequence of the emergency, if things carry on as they are, is 'Hothouse Earth', uninhabitable by humans and millions of other species certainly, but a physical condition of uninhabitability. This is what we need to know. So the warning of the climate emergency, supported by the empirical measurement of the Earth's 'vital signs', spells out in the clearest metrics of risk, the physical processes that are destabilising the Earth System. Thus, even given the consumption of renewable energy (solar, wind) increasing almost 4 times over a decade, it was still 28 times less than the consumption of fossil fuels. In spite of the Paris Treaty (undermined as it has been by Trump's withdrawal from it, aped by Bolsonaro in Brazil), CO_2 emissions rose from 400 parts per million (ppm) in 2015 to a peak of nearly 415 ppm in 2019. Charting the level and pace of change from 1980 to the present day, on every significant indicator there is no flattening of the upward curve, whether it concerns the various greenhouse gases (carbon dioxide, methane, nitrous oxide), world human population, numbers of ruminant livestock and per capita meat consumption, surface sea temperature, sea level changes, oceanic heat content change, air passenger miles, or extreme weather events. Conceived of as the Earth's biophysical system, the world is pushing from risk to irreversible change at every significant planetary boundary, risking cascades of tipping points. That is indeed an Earth System emergency.

The scientists who have developed these concepts of 'the anthropogenic' Anthropocene, Planetary Boundaries, and the 'safe operating space for humanity' are clearly aware of what they are doing and what they are not doing. They can also be quite outspoken about their judgement of what social and political sciences are not doing.

> *The predominant paradigm of social and economic development remains largely oblivious to the risk of human-induced environmental disasters at continental to planetary scales.*
>
> (Rockström et al., 2009)

Thus, also, they present 'humanity's challenge' in terms of various physical fixes, cuts in greenhouse gas emissions, increases in carbon sinks, or solar radiation management. It is summed up in the optimistic if rather fantastic vision in which 'humanity plays an active planetary stewardship role in maintaining a state intermediate between the glacial-interglacial limit cycle of the Late Quaternary and a Hothouse Earth' (Steffen et al., 2018, p. 8256). It is a humanity devoid of politics, nation states, particular economic organisation, or cultures. What makes one fear that it is only a fantasy vision is that this abstract humanity is not a present or credible agent for change, however impressive the school strikes and social movements. If only humanity could make its presence felt.

Given what we know about the Earth System climate emergency, it is manifestly at one and the same time, a political, economic, societal and cultural emergency. The UN COP25 conference held in Madrid in 2019, the most recent and important international political climate change event, has been described as fiddling while the planet burns (Newell & Taylor, 2020). Literally. Unprecedented Australian bush fires followed the politically licensed burning of vast swathes of the Amazon. Where the political responses to the Covid-19 pandemic, however inadequate and laggardly, have occurred at a speed and urgency that have cut emissions from world transport at a stroke, the longer term political responses to climate change have signally failed to flatten *any* of the multiple upward curves just described.

Compared with the resources, international collaborations, and UN support and investment in the natural science of climate change, social science developments have been relatively meagre and under-resourced. Given the political character of the climate emergency, in particular the failure to achieve global coordination between radically different, often conflicting, societal interests, that deficit is a major obstacle to meeting the challenge.

There is – at least as yet or on the horizon – no super science of complex system interactions, embracing both the Earth System as a physical system and historical, socioeconomic processes of change. And this book will certainly not provide one, or even attempt one. Nonetheless, given the present separation and division of labour, it is important to take as much cognisance of each other's work as possible.

The central argument of this book is that in order to understand the contemporary political and societal climate emergency, we need an understanding of the historical processes that got the world into such a fix. The societal differences that now impede international climate change mitigation are the outcome of long and varied historical processes. The organising concept is the **sociogenesis** of climate change, and consequently, an analysis of how societies have made a crisis into an emergency. Sociogenesis is offered as a complementary counterpart rather than a substitute for, let alone critique of, the natural scientific concepts of anthropogenesis and the Anthropocene.

This chapter presents the concept of sociogenesis in its bare bones, to be fleshed out and developed through the course of the book. Firstly, it will be placed in conversation with other approaches, notably Marxist ones, that in broad terms analyse the climate emergency as the result of capitalism's unbridled, largely unregulated, exploitation of Nature. These approaches undoubtedly present a powerful social scientific case that links the climate crisis with the emergence of industrial capitalism. It is a case to be listened and responded to rather than dismissed (Chapter 2). Secondly, the concept is developed in relation to the major historical changes that have already been referred to as 'the great divergence' (Chapter 3), notably the British industrial revolution and the colonisation of the New World. Then taking a particular empirical example of recent times, a contrast is drawn between China and Brazil, and the dynamics of the production of food, and what is generating societally contrasting transitions to eating more meat. The sociogenic transformations of these two societies are polar opposites, and yet, through trade between them, the book will show how opposites attract. That particular 'marriage' is one which makes its own distinctive contribution to the climate emergency – not one party or the other, but the marriage itself (Chapter 4).

Thirdly, different societies inhabit different fossil and renewable energy resource environments in a manner which has shaped not only their own historical developments, but also international divisions and conflicts in the world. These are at the heart of the sociogenic dynamics of fossil energy driven climate change (Chapter 5).

Running through these examples, inequalities over the rights to exploit and consume earth's resources both between and within nations are at the very centre of the sociogenesis of climate change. National historical developments are diverse in both their productive systems and patterns of consumption in ways that generate climate change. The poor, in whatever country, have a fraction of the climate impact of the rich. But, as with the example of China and Brazil, or indeed the production and consumption of oil, the analysis needs to combine the generation of unequal exploitation of earth's resources in production with unequal enjoyment of those resources in consumption (Chapter 6).

The concept of sociogenesis is thus developed both conceptually and empirically in the course of the book, which will culminate in drawing out the political implications for addressing the climate emergency (Chapter 7). In doing so, this is *not* world history, but takes a much more limited few steps by exploring some aspects of the historical development of climate change. As already indicated, it merely demonstrates the need to rewrite history backwards through the lens of climate change. Classically, the British industrial revolution and the emergence of empire have been analysed as an economic, political and cultural transformation of revolutionary proportions, rather than in terms of its specific dynamic of climate change. Similarly, colonisation of the New World, and then the American Revolutionary War with the independent trajectory of the development of the United States as a settler colonising society have not been fully appreciated for their ecological transformational significance. The chunk by chunk, state by state, geographical expansion and occupation of a continent had its own historical trajectory, its self-proclaimed 'manifest destiny', to exploit the environmental resources on a continental scale.

So what is sociogenesis? It is a concept that arises from an economic sociology approach that has its origins in the later works of Karl Polanyi. Writing in the mid-twentieth century before significance of climate change had come into prominence, Polanyi himself argued that the unregulated domination of markets, if allowed to continue, would threaten the sustainability of the environment and the health of human beings. The market logic of reducing human beings and natural resources to commodities, where only the financial gains from market exchanges prevailed, would destroy the land and lead to the unrestrained exploitation of labour, from childhood to death. His view of nature was that its benefits to humanity were inherently not man-made, and that to reduce all those benefits to commodities for sale is ultimately self-destructive.

But Polanyi's world was shaped by two world wars, by the experience of the rise of Nazism and fascism, and by the conflicts between socialist and capitalist polities and societies. Unsurprisingly, his views on the self-destructiveness of human expropriations of nature remained underdeveloped. His most famous work, *The Great Transformation*, focuses on the rise to dominance of the unregulated market in the period of the

British industrial revolution. It was written from an historical
vantage point of the world emerging from the Second World
War. It could not have written about the great transformation
from a climate change perspective. He lived in a present that
was just not there.

In his later works, he turned to comparative historical and
anthropological studies of the shifting place of the economy in
society. In the broadest of terms, he contrasted societies where
society (including culture and moral norms) and polity
dominated the economy to the market societies of today
where economies dominate the society and polity. This work
was saying of the present world, where human relations are
reduced to transactional market thinking (gains and losses),
that social and economic life does not have to be like that.
There is nothing universal about the dominance of economies
or market logics and moralities as the dictating principles of
our social lives. It is a radical idea of how economies are
instituted differently in different societies.

The idea of sociogenesis takes this radical idea one major step
further. It argues that societies, and within them their economies, are instituted differently in different natural resource
environments. Conceptually, it is the shift from Fig. 1.1 to
Fig. 1.2.

Polanyi argued that the economy 'shifted place' within
society, in relation to social norms and morals, in more recent
times often formalised into laws, shaped and influenced by
different religious cultures and different political systems. That
is represented in Fig. 1.1. This vision of the shifting place of
the economy in society is then critically placed in the diverse
spatial contexts of environmental resources (sun, water, coal,
soil, climate) with which societies interact and develop. That is
the conceptual shift in Fig. 1.2. We need to make this shift in
perspective to understand how societies generate climate
change.

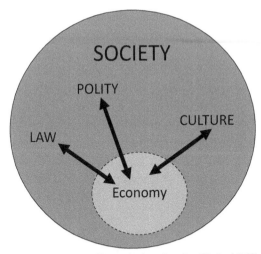

Fig. 1.1. Polanyi: How Economies Are Instituted Differently in Different Societies.

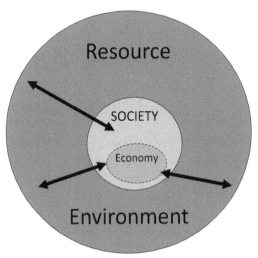

Fig. 1.2. How Societies (+Economies) Are Instituted Differently in Different Resource Environments.

In the light of this shift, let us briefly reconsider the debates within the natural sciences about when the Anthropocene began and by what anthropogenic processes, the Long View and the industrial revolution 'short' view. Little can be known about the transformation of hunter gatherer societies into settled agriculturalist rice cultivators in the Yangtse River Basin 6,500 years ago. But we can be certain that it was a major socio-economic transformation, including in what we would now describe as the economic activity of food provisioning and corresponding cultures of consumption. Carbon-dated evidence of the spread of irrigated rice agriculture however clearly indicates that it occurred in very specific resource environments in terms of topologies, climate and surface water. Moreover, as the ice-cores demonstrate, it had its distinctive greenhouse gas signature, methane. Carbon-dated evidence of the spread of domesticated livestock, although no doubt with similar methane emissions, displays a radically different spatial distribution, embracing Africa, much of India, and the northern plains of China. Again, a radical transformation of socio-economies developed in specific resource environments, with climate atmospheric consequences. The domestication of arable crops, and its subsequent spread through deforestation in Northern Europe, has a different spatial imprint, notably in the Middle East, and a different greenhouse gas impact, in this case predominantly CO_2 (Fuller et al., 2011; Ruddiman, 2013).

As will be discussed more fully below (Chapter 3), an important part of the explanation of why the industrial revolution initially emerged in Great Britain was the presence in its immediate resource environment of the right kind of coal at the right price. Great Britain had already shifted to coal for domestic heating in contrast to much of continental Europe reliant on peat (Allen, 2009). It was a socio-economy sitting on top of a significant coal resource. The concept of sociogenesis, rooted in how socio-economies are instituted in particular resource environments, or extend their control over them through colonisation or acquisitions of trade, thus embraces both the Long View of the origins of climate change and the shorter Industrialisation View dating from the mid-eighteenth century. It provides a unifying conceptual framework, covering industrial and pre-industrial societies.

Moreover, the shorter view provides a starting line and a starting gun (Watt's steam engine again), from a socio-historical perspective. However, that starting line presumes the social, economic and political transformations in Britain that preceded it, notably the enclosure of land and changes in property rights, the loss of the commons, and an agricultural revolution. In short, within a sociogenesis perspective it makes no sense to think of a ground zero starting point, of climate change just beginning from scratch. Any period of transition is preceded by previous transitions. That is history. Put crudely, the industrial revolution in the eighteenth century could not have occurred without the prior domestication of crops and livestock many thousands of years previously. Sociogenesis is a continuous and varied historical process.

In addition to the natural science perspectives on the Long View versus the Industrialisation View, the other key set of concepts examined here are the consideration of planetary boundaries and the physical and biological complexity of the Earth System as a system. Again the concept of sociogenesis complements rather than replaces this perspective, in two major ways, in terms of where and how different societies inhabit the planet, and in terms of how socio-economic inequalities contribute to the climate emergency.

Societies, and in particular, national states do not inhabit the planet in any uniform way. Societies are instituted in geographical space. They are sited in their own immediate resource environments, with their own localised if shifting boundaries, restricting or expanding. It matters whether they are in the tropics, the temperate zone, or the Arctic Circle. It matters if they have the Amazon in their back gardens or huge reserves of coal or oil in their cellars. Although these statistics will need to be revisited, it comes as little surprise that those countries with major oil or coal reserves today rank highly as responsible for national greenhouse gas emissions (e.g. Saudi Arabia, Australia, UAE, and Iran). Never mind the political turbulence and wars in the Middle East over oil (Mitchell, 2011), the First and Second World Wars and their aftermaths saw state boundaries being contested and redrawn, notably between France and Germany, or Germany and Poland, over territorial control of coal resources. Even Chile and Peru engaged in a guano war that resulted in Chile acquiring Peru's rich nitrogen resource. It also matters if states project their economic and political power through colonisation or trade. British imperialism, in particular, emerged at a particular historical period, with a unique spatial fix across distinct regions of the globe to become the most significant climate change game changer of that epoch (Chapter 3). It is important to name it, to look at history backwards through the climate change perspective. The British Empire was more than a spatially political and economic hegemonic power. It was *at the same time* a climate changer. As Fig. 1.2 suggests, how different nation states interact with the natural resource environments over which they have spatial control is critical for understanding climate change.

Socio-economic inequalities also impose a different perspective on how to understand planetary boundaries socio-scientifically. As we have seen, planetary boundaries are metrics that measure the aggregate impacts of human activity. But, as always, aggregates mask socio-economic inequalities. The world scientists' climate emergency warning deals in aggregates, and ranks the top 25 countries in terms of the biggest aggregate emissions of CO_2 (Ripple, Wolf, Newsome, Barnard, & Moomaw, 2019, Supplemental Table S1). Unsurprisingly, China, with a population of 1.4 billion comes top. Yet, if instead countries are ranked in terms of per capita emissions, China drops to ninth below the USA, Europe, Japan, Australia, Singapore, Canada, the UAE. As we shall analyse in greater depths in Chapter 6, CO_2 emissions per capita closely track wealth, crudely measured by GDP per capita. The average Chinese citizen produces two and a half times less CO_2 than the average American, and produces over six times less GDP. The contrasts are even greater where the inequalities are greater. The average American is 16 times wealthier than the average Indian and produces over 9 times more CO_2. Moreover, these societal averages of course mask inequalities within countries. And there are super-rich people in most of the top 25 countries. It has been calculated that the top 10% of the wealthiest people world-wide contribute 45% of greenhouse gas emissions, where the bottom 50% of the least wealthy contribute only 13% (Oxfam, 2015; Chancel & Piketty, 2015).

Planetary boundary analysis measures the aggregate impacts of human activity but, as we have seen, also sets thresholds and boundaries. A sociogenic inequalities perspective completely alters the way to see the risks of transgressing these limits by considering the wealth inequality characteristics of 'the human'. The International Panel on Climate Change has now suggested an imperative of not overshooting a 1.5°C global warming, resetting the agenda for avoiding the climate emergency (IPCC, 2018). To achieve this, it requires aggregate 'humanity' to reduce carbon emissions by 45% of 2010 levels by 2030, and to reach net carbon zero by 2050. Many argue that the pace of decarbonisation has to start quicker and end earlier. Nonetheless, taking those figures would mean reducing the global average per capita CO_2 from their current 4.4 CO_2

tonnes equivalent to 2.4 CO_2 tonnes equivalent. That is for the average planetary human. But if we look at the average American, it would require a reduction from their current level of 15.7 CO_2 tonnes equivalent, compared with the average Chinese from their current level of 6.5 CO_2 tonnes equivalent, or the average European 6.8 CO_2 tonnes equivalent. Again, these are national averages, but show the hugely varied societal challenges for achieving 1.5°C global warming by 2030. The top 1% of global wealthy individuals, whether in the USA or China, Europe, India or Brazil, have a slightly greater task awaiting them. They have been calculated to have a current level of 200 CO_2 tonnes equivalent per capita of emissions. They need to reduce their burning of greenhouse gases 100 times if they are going to contribute equally to addressing the climate emergency. Can or will the rich abandon their wealthy lifestyles to save the planet? Staying at the national level, and considering the scale of the inequalities challenge to meet the climate emergency, several major economies in the top 25 countries for greenhouse gas emissions have per capita emissions well *below* the global average target reduction for 2030, notably India, Pakistan, Egypt, Indonesia and Brazil. The per capita wealth gaps, within and between countries are fundamental to understanding the climate crisis. Planetary thresholds are transgressed beyond all scientific boundaries by the super-rich, while poverty restricts millions from enjoying even basic environmental resources, such as safe drinking water. Wealth inequalities generate massively different greenhouse gas impacts on the Earth's System, and at the same time present a major obstacle and multiple resistances to taking the decisive political action to address the climate emergency.

This initial introduction of the concept of sociogenesis of climate change embraces a number of dimensions which will be explored through the course of the book. It is an integrative concept that combines the political, economic, social and cultural social processes resulting in climate change as well as those blocking its prevention or mitigation. At the centre of the concept is the idea of socio-economies being instituted in, and interacting with, the resource environments over which they have a political and economic reach. In this book, the focus is on the sociogenesis of climate change. Elsewhere, it has been used to analyse the sustainability crises over the exploitation and pollution of water resources, and the provision of safe drinking water (Harvey, 2015). As suggested at the opening of the book, it can also be deployed to analyse the development and spread of a pandemic, including the present one. Reflecting on the sociogenic causes of a pandemic and on sociogenic causes of the climate emergency, understanding their *differences*, improves understanding all round. A classic example of this approach, although the author does not use the term sociogenesis, is the analysis of cholera epidemics in Europe in the late nineteenth century. Richard Evans compares Hamburg, which suffered extremely high levels of mortality, unevenly distributed between rich and poor, between rich merchants and their domestic servants, with the neighbouring city in Prussia, Altona, where mortality was very low (Evans, 1990). Public investment in water infrastructures in one city contrasted with lack of it in the other because of resistance from commercial interests. Disputes between scientists over how the disease was spread, and how the lethal bacillus was socially introduced and then spread unevenly across the cities, played a critical role. Prussia pursued state-interventionist politics, imposed quarantines, and regulated medical professions, while Hamburg, an independent Free City, promoted the free market and individual choice over how people look after their bodies, making no qualification requirements for anyone to practice medicine. It was a story of death in Hamburg, life in Altona. The comparisons between then and now resonate quite strikingly. So, although a sociogenesis analysis of the COVID-19 is yet to be done, it already shows why we need to have a sociogenic approach to understand why decisive political actions have taken place in some countries and to varying degrees for the pandemic, while anything but decisive political actions have been taken to address climate change.

In the next chapter, the sociogenic concept is developed further when discussing primarily Marxist ways of analysing the climate change emergency. In some ways the Marxist view chimes most closely with the natural science short history vision of climate change being triggered by the emergence of industrial capitalism. Some have therefore argued against the concept of the Anthropocene, re-naming it the Capitalocene. It is capitalism what done it. The fact that there is this corre-spondence between a social science and a natural science perspective demands that these social science accounts of climate change be fully considered. To date within the social sciences, Marxist accounts stand out for grasping the scale and complexity of how political economies generate climate change. As already argued, however, the sociogenesis perspective adopts an integrative view including pre-industrial and industrial capitalist forms of sociogenesis. It aims to go beyond Marxist analyses with an analysis which is much more radically historical and spatial, eschewing all abstract models of 'the economy'. Rather it stresses how economies are insti-tuted and continuously reconfigured, politically and legally, in varying ways across environmental space and historical time.

The historical and comparative chapters that follow sub-stantiate this conceptual analysis, emphasising the diverse historical trajectories that, in combination, have generated the climate emergency. Indeed it is precisely the diversity and the inequalities between and within societies, generated by these histories that matter. These histories weigh heavily on the present, contributing to the political complexities of address-ing the climate emergency. But this book is not, and indeed cannot be, a political manifesto for the world. The sociogenic approach rather points to the need to develop distinctive politics at different scales, the local, through to the national and the international. Different societies, with their historical legacies, face very different challenges. One of the limitations of the UN hosted climate conferences, including Paris and COP21, was that they only required producer nations to propose national development plans for climate change miti-gation. Neither the inequalities between nations, nor the sig-nificance of the varied links between producer nations and consumer nations manifest in the global links of international trade, have been fully addressed. The climate politics of trade in relation to climate change are buried under the silence of the World Trade Organisation. A sociogenic analysis provides only a grounding for developing politics of inequality and climate change, and of different societal politics arising from histories of interactions between polities and the resource environments over which they extend their exploitation.

2

A TWENTY-FIRST-CENTURY HISTORICAL MATERIALISM FIT FOR THE CLIMATE EMERGENCY

From the evidence of natural scientists, it is clear that something about human activity occurred in the course of the eighteenth and nineteenth centuries that radically changed the Earth's atmosphere. Theirs is an analysis of the aggregating and enduring *impacts* of human activity on the Earth's System. Asking what this human activity was and is concerns rather the political, socioeconomic and cultural processes *producing* these impacts. The question becomes what lies behind the 'genesis' in the natural scientists' anthropogenesis.

Something called 'the industrial revolution' occurred and with it industrial capitalism, the emergence of urban proletariats working in factories across Europe and North America. As we have seen, this take-off has been attributed to the use of coal as a fossil energy forging iron and steel, producing machinery and then powering that machinery, both in factories and in railway transport. It also contributed to the revolution in chemicals derived from coal. However, as will be examined in greater detail (Chapter 5), coal as a source of energy was itself further revolutionised by its use in the generation of electricity, both for industrial and domestic use. And then, as a further accelerant of Earth's atmospheric change, oil in all its uses added a huge new source of fossil energy emitting CO_2 into the atmosphere. This was not just one technological event or phase of innovation centred on the steam engine that broke with the past. There were waves upon waves of transformational change, each with different trajectories in different countries, politically, socially and economically.

> *So, what lies behind the genesis of climate change?*
>
> *It's the Capitalocene, stupid!*
>
> *From the Industrial Revolution, a new era begins: the earth under the rule of capital and capital under the rule of the most powerful imperialists.*
>
> (Altvater, 2016)

In global terms, it is argued that a relatively small handful of capitalists owning and continuously transforming the means of production, seeking profit, competing to create and dominate markets, and above all accumulating capital on an expanding scale, changed the Earth's climate, irreversibly. Given the scale of both this transformation, and of its impact on the Earth System, Marx identified and theorised capitalism as a historically revolutionary mode of production. It was an analysis which grasped the scale and societal breadth of change, displacing and superseding previously existing modes of economic organisation, notably European feudalism and oriental despotism. His was a grand and historical materialist understanding of the major transformations of social forma-tions. But his was not, and indeed could not have been, a theory of how political economies generate climate change. To think otherwise is to commit an absurd anachronism. Climate change calls for a radically revised historical materialism that grasps how socioeconomic transformations at the same time transform the earth's atmosphere and planetary sustainability for human social life and the life of other species.

Nonetheless, there have been valiant and insightful attempts to squeeze new environmental wine into old theoretical bottles. In developing the concept of sociogenesis, a dialogue with these Marxist attempts is intended not to reject but to go beyond a conception of the economy which needs fundamental re-visioning in order to do the work of understanding the genesis of climate change. Put at its very simplest, Marx was attempting to theorise what constitutes 'the economy' in the midst of a maelstrom of radical transformation, and developed an abstract model of a closed circuit capital-labour-commodity economy oiled by monetary exchanges. He was defining a new mode of production as the pre-eminent reality of his time, riven with contradictions, witnessing new class relations and conflict, and last but by no means least, creating the social forces – the industrial proletariat – that might have the capacity to overthrow a regime of intensifying exploitation. Climate change, or, as we shall see, even with his undoubted perception of environmental degradation, was not first, second or third in the political agenda. But it is now. In order to appreciate the new realities of the climate emergency, Marx's old conceptions of what is meant by 'the economy of Capital' need to be understood for their limitations as much for their positive yield. Here is not the place to undertake the broader critique of Marx's conception of the workings of the economy as represented in the three volumes of *Capital*, the *Grundrisse* or *Theories of Surplus Value* (see Harvey & Geras, 2018). Aside from climate change, there are other realities that Marx, by virtue of his mid-nineteenth century historical standpoint, could not have theorised and which demand radical revision of the very foundations of his theory, notably the emergence of mass education and the reproduction of labour power through learning and teaching rather than simply the socially necessary consumption of market commodities. Here the focus is strictly on developing a historical materialist conception of the economy fit for grasping the genesis of climate emergency. The fundamental question to be addressed is how to understand capitalist political economies, in their spatial and historical specificities, as driving climate change. And, more bluntly, is there an overriding contradiction between the imperatives of those economies and planetary sustainability?

Four concepts of environmental Marxists stand out for consideration in respect to these questions:

1. capitalism as programmed ecological self-destruction;

2. the Capitalocene as a new geological epoch;

3. the metabolic rift between capitalist society and nature;

4. the unequal exchange between industrial metropolises and environmental resources of less developed economies.

SELF-DESTRUCTING CAPITALISM

Even before climate change came to dominate the greening of Marxism, an influential current of thinking proposed that capitalism – unlike any previous social formation – had the proclivity to undermine the very conditions of its own development.[1] Drawing on Polanyi's perspective discussed in

---

1 In a series of essays in ecological Marxism dating from between 1988-1998, it is striking that warming of the earth's atmosphere makes only a fleeting appearance (O'Connor, 1998, p. 166).

chapter one, the pursuit of profit and accumulation of capital is contained within a model of the economy which *in its internal logic* excludes any consideration of natural limits or barriers.

> *The combined power of capitalist production relations and productive forces self-destruct by impairing or destroying rather than reproducing their own conditions.*

(O'Connor, 1998, p. 165)

This tendency to self-destruct is based on some fundamental assumptions about what constitutes 'the economy' of market commodities. At the very core of this analysis is Marx's proposition that what underlies all value in market exchanges – exchange value – is the amount of labour time necessary for its production. Labour – ultimately – creates value underpinning the relative prices of products in the market. On the basis of this foundational proposition, a theory is built on how profits are made, how capital is created, and the division between those that own capital and those who have only their labour to sell. Here is not the place to dig deeper into the complexities of this analysis. The critical conceptual move for present purposes is the one already flagged: exchange value is created by labour alone in terms of quanta of abstract labour time, a time measurement applicable to all kinds of labour no matter its qualitative differences. Anything not produced by labour falls outside this framing of what distinctively constitutes a capitalist economy. In this conception, nature, the environment, the atmosphere, human biology, water, coal, 'raw' materials in their untouched state, cannot *have or produce* exchange value in themselves because they are not produced by labour. In a sense, the fact that plants or animals grow of themselves, biologically, or that coal has a specific calorific potential derived from trapping solar energy, is a free gift of nature. Being unproduced by human labour, their natural virtues are assumed to provide cheap, even costless, benefits to humans unless through over-exploitation they become scarce or damaged.

All transformations of these natural externalities are of economic significance for the development of capitalism only insofar as they add the labour time element, no matter how. And, for capitalism, it does not matter how. In this view, the economy by its nature is prone to destroy nature, those very environmental characteristics, including human biological life, that are the very conditions of its own growth and continuity. The pursuit of the creation of more and more exchange value, and with it profit and capital accumulation, occurs regardless of its effects on the quality of biological life and the physical environment. The economic dynamic of capitalism, once historically set in motion, expands beyond any territorial or biological boundaries, universalises across the globe, detaching itself from any roots in localised environments. It confronts Nature in general, as its domain to plunder for all the free gifts on offer.[2] From the depths of the Amazon forest to the bottom of the deepest oceans. Or nitrogen in the atmosphere.

In this conceptualisation of the capitalist economy, the logic of exchange value is, if unrestrained, ultimately self-destructive. On top of the central contradiction of capitalism and its proneness to economically self-destruct through over-production and under-consumption under its regime of economic exploitation, there is thus a second contradiction: its proneness to ecologically self-destruct under its regime of environmental exploitation. Just as the politics of class conflict emerges as a consequence of the first contradiction, so

---

2 'Natural elements entering as agents into production, and which cost nothing, no matter what role they play in production do not enter as components of capital, but as a free gift of Nature to capital, that is, as a free gift of Nature's productive power to labour...' Marx, Capital, III, 745.

environmental and social movements, and the critical role of the state in intermediating between capital and nature, emerge as a consequence of the second contradiction. Economic and environmental exploitation are welded together in the logic of exchange value.

This is a powerful conceptual vision of the interaction between capitalism-in-general and global Nature, providing a particular account of environmental disasters of all kinds, atmospheric warming, toxic wastes, air pollution, soil degradation, plastic dumping, species extinctions...an endless and growing list. It is unquestionably a conceptualisation fit for the scale of the historical transformation of the earth's atmosphere evident from the epoch of the industrial revolution.

THE CAPITALOCENE

So, now in the shadow of the climate emergency, is it appropriate, and how does it add to the analysis, to speak of the Capitalocene? The concept of the Capitalocene emerged as a direct response and challenge to the natural scientific concept of the Anthropocene, and its widespread popularisation. The rejection of the natural science concept on occasion could scarcely be more provocative:

> *The Anthropocene has become the most important –*
> *and also the most dangerous – environmental*
> *concept of our times.*
>
> (Moore, 2018, p. 237)

The twin concept of anthropogenic climate change is equally condemned as a colossal falsification, and in its place:

> *Global warming is capital's crowning achievement.*
> *Global warming is* capitalogenic.
>
> (Moore, 2018, p. 237)

By replacing Anthropocene with Capitalocene and anthro-pogenic with capitalogenic it is striking that the concept retains the framing of a geological epoch rather than replacing it by historical time, the capitalist epoch or era. It is perhaps equally striking that, in general, the capitalocene is not theorised as a modification of the geological interglacial cycle of the Holo-cene, which tends to disappear off the analytical scene. As we shall see, in some versions, the concept of Capitalocene contests any reference to a Nature outside of human society, in its rejection of any human society abstracted from the 'web of life' on earth. To do so commits the sin of dualism, opposing Society to Nature.

The principal ambition of this conceptual shift is to contest a view that climate change is induced by human beings *in general*, even human societies *in general*. Pitting humanity in the abstract against Nature is founded on a flawed dualism, so the argument goes. Additionally, natural scientists are accused of treating population growth as such, the multiplication of humans, as a factor of climate change, rather than population growth within systems of power and economy. Finally, evocation of Watt's steam engine by the natural scientists as responsible for the concept of the Anthropocene is attacked for taking a technology out of its context of industrial capitalism – and by implication any further climate-changing technologies – and putting it in the hands of humanity in general.

The Capitalocene replaces the Anthropocene and in so doing treats the decisive shift towards climate change as occurring with the historical emergence of capitalism. Amongst those who deploy the concept of Capitalocene, the immediate question arises, when does this capitalism begin, and in particular when does its beginning become significant for climate change. As with natural scientists, although on an altogether much shorter timescale, there is a longer view and a shorter view. The longer view sets the beginning at around 1450, and it is the one to be considered here first. The shorter view argues, with natural scientists, that the decisive shift came with the adoption of coal and steam power – broadly the industrial revolution – from around the turn of the nineteenth century. The difference, however, is not just one of timing, but entails significant differences in the concept of the Capitalocene, which need to be clarified.

The longer view situates the emergence of the Capitalocene in the mid-fifteenth century as a combination of economic, political, and cultural shift from within an expanding natural environment. The shift thus has several critical components that are not just narrowly economic in character. Pioneering research examined how the expansion of European capitalism Westwards, eventually into the New World, at the same time involved a re-organisation of nature (Moore, 2009, 2010). Exemplary in this respect was the move Westwards of sugar production, first heralded by Sydney Mintz (Mintz, 1986). The island of Madeira witnessed an expansion of the sugar 'commodity frontier', on the one hand, and the generation of an ecological disaster on the other, notably a deforestation that was progressive and ultimately self-destructive. The establishment of slave plantation sugar on 'the island of wood' (Madeira = wood) involved not only initial deforestation for planting, but more significantly as time progressed over the next century, an ever increasing demand for burning wood required in sugar refining. The costs in time and labour necessary to obtain diminishing forest resources further and further away from the sugar refining 'factories in the fields', rendered Madeiran sugar uncompetitive. The commodity frontier then crossed the Atlantic, first to Brazil and then to the Caribbean, with the final stages of sugar refining in the metropolitan countries shifting North to rely on Baltic timber imports. Madeira itself was almost denuded of forest: its name lost its claim.

Paradigmatic of semi-industrialised agriculture and the expansion of commodity production for an ever expanding market, the Madeiran self-destructive ecological disaster is not presented primarily as a significant climate changing event in itself, but heralding a new era. Notably from Columbus and the colonisation of the New World, the idea of ever expanding commodity frontiers enlarged hugely on the concept already discussed of Nature's free gifts. The colonisation of the Americas opened up two continents-full of natural bounty. Capitalism was reorganising world ecology as it appropriated and then exhausted Nature's free gifts, only to move the frontier ever onwards and outwards.

Whether the frontiers were strictly territorial (e.g. New World) or geological (e.g. coal, oil), the expanding commodity frontiers in this conception of the Capitalocene provided the new capitalist-in-nature four 'cheaps': food, labour, energy and raw materials. The term 'cheap' is confusing, inasmuch as nature's provisions are either free in which case they are not cheap, or somehow have an exchange value in themselves, just a lower one than would have been required had wage labour produced these 'gifts'. The confusion is intensified by the inclusion of non-paid labour – child care for example – as free, although clearly involving human labour, and not a 'gift of nature'. The confusion is exacerbated yet further by the inclusion of plantation slavery, portrayed mistakenly as the cheap alternative to wage labour, with slaves being treated as chattels as if they were natural animals like cattle (Moore, 2017, pp. 11, 19). Slavery never emerged as the alternative to wage labour because it was cheaper, but as an essential source of labour for expanding plantation economies, following failures to enslave indigenous peoples or recruit sufficient indentured white labour from Europe. Moreover, from the initial violence of capture, through the Middle Passage to the violence of coerced labour on the plantations, slavery can be analytically bracketed together with so-called nature's free gifts only as an act of conceptual violence.

Putting such confusions aside, however, the theory of the four cheaps and expanding commodity frontiers argues that capitalism generates its own ecological crisis, one of declining rates of growth and profit. Cheapness declines with the exhaustion of new commodity frontiers; with limits to ever increasing agricultural productivity being reached; and with 'free labour' becoming a diminishing resource. These are not natural limits, but capitalism's natural limits, within its world ecological system. The 'end of the four cheaps' heralds the demise of the capitalist world ecology, and as such represents a substantial re-working of the concept of self-destruction discussed above. At this point, to be taken up again later, it is worth signalling that the end of the four cheaps is in many ways a concept still tied into the primary contradiction, the *economic* rather than ecological self-destruction of capitalism. Surprisingly little attention is paid to the generation of climate change as such and the consequent rendering of the planet as uninhabitable. Rather the capitalist world ecology becomes more and more unprofitable, unexploitable (Moore, 2014).

Nonetheless, the critique of the dangerous concept of the Anthropocene and its replacement by the Capitalocene proposes that capitalism itself treats nature as an infinitely exploitable reality external to the economy of abstract labour and exchange value. This capital-nature dualism of the long view is linked to the profound cultural shift that saw emergent science from the Renaissance onwards as treating Nature as a separate sphere of scientific objectivity, to be studied as such. For the long view, the symbolic figure is Descartes as the epitome of this dualistic thinking, the counterpart to James Watt for the short view.

> *The capitalist revolution...turned on the Cartesian revolution.*

(Moore, 2017, p. 12)

The Cartesian revolution in turn is held responsible for the purposive control of nature by the application of science, leading to a 'rationality of world conquest and domination' (Moore, 2017, p. 12). The economic dualism of capitalism-nature in this perspective is thus integral to the society-nature dualism of scientific thinking, the very dualism of which the concept of Anthropocene is held to be so dangerous. At times this concept borders on a critique of natural science as such, invoking the idea of a super-knowledge integrating the social-in-the-natural, the natural-in-the social, a unifying knowledge of the Web of Life (Moore, 2015).

This long view version of the concept of the Capitalocene has two paradoxical consequences. Having set its stall out against the natural science concept of the Anthropocene, very little attention is paid to those Earth System effects as analysed by natural science, how significant and in what ways the period prior to industrialisation was for global warming, species extinctions, tipping points, little ice ages and bubonic plague. At the same time, a generic capitalism reigns world-wide from 1450 onwards, with no period-isation, no national or political variations. In spite of a rich and extensive list of expanding incorporation of nature into the ecology of global capitalism (silver, potash, Baltic timber, coal, iron, copper), there is an appearance of seamless continuity. In finality, conceptually the Capitalocene is characterised by a generic capitalism within an ecology of abstract nature.

> *The dialectic of abstract nature and abstract labour is*
> *at the heart of those historical natures that are cause,*
> *consequence and unfolding condition of world*
> *accumulation.*

(Moore, 2018, p. 254)

In this conception, what is meant by abstract nature is on the one hand the subjection of the free gifts of nature in all their qualitative diversity to the single measure of money in the market, through their appropriation by abstract labour. On the other, it is nature abstracted from all social relations as grasped by natural scientists: mapped, measured, quantified and experimented with – all with the consequence of rendering nature exploitable. The Capitalocene is ultimately a conception of the incorporation of the world in the capitalist 'web of life', not of the genesis of climate change. The long view Capitalocene and the Anthropocene are not talking about the same planet.

By contrast the shorter view of the Capitalocene is directly and specifically addressing climate change, aligning itself with the natural scientists by taking the rapid acceleration of CO_2 emissions as the key moment in the human impact on the Earth system's atmosphere. Moreover, the rapid acceleration is attributed to the burning of coal and steam power used in industrial manufacture. The analysis then does what natural scientists do not do, going beyond a technology that generates the impacts to grasp what drives the development and appropriation of that technology. It focuses down onto what was happening in Britain at a specific place and time, and especially on the transition from a non-climate change use of energy – water power – to a climate-change inducing use of energy, fossil coal and steam power (Malm, 2016).

Simplifying a complex and detailed historical account, steam power replaced water power not because of any technical superiority or relative cost (which was arguably higher). Steam power won out because competing textile capitalists were resistant to collaborating with each other or a public authority in order to invest in the necessary water power infrastructures as a collective resource. Moreover, water power was often located in rural areas at a distance from labour markets and consumer markets, both concentrated in towns. This made recruitment and retention of factory wage labour more difficult, and access to domestic and export markets for textiles more logistically complex. In short, steam power was more concordant with individual capitalist entrepreneurial factories employing a nascent urban proletariat. Even more summarily, burning fossil fuel was a capitalist solution to energy use and manufacturing. The spike of the mid-nineteenth century was tied directly to the emergence of a distinctively capitalist organisation of industry. Hence, climate change is capitalogenic, with the capitalist owners of the textile mills (the means of production) as its principal agents.

Almost as an opposite argument to the 'nature's free gift' conception of the long view Capitalocene, the free gifts of water power and gravity were rejected in favour of the much more labour intensive energy source of mined and transported coal. In this short view of the Capitalocene, therefore, climate change is seen to be induced by a particular form of industrial capitalism, located spatially in England and Scotland, and historically timed with the observed acceleration in CO_2 emissions. In 1825, Britain contributed 80% of CO_2 emissions from burning coal, and still as much as 62% in 1850 (Malm, 2016). In mid-century, Britain was emitting twice as much CO_2 as the United States, France, Germany and Belgium combined. In its detailed historical account of the transition from water to steam power, the analysis provides a refreshing contrast with the treatment of abstract nature. The rivers and gradients that had driven the water mills of the early textile industrialisation had a specific geography and natural quality, and the availability of the right kind of coal within relatively short transportable distances provided Britain with a distinctive comparative advantage. The story is one of a distinctively British resource environment, not one of generic capitalism and abstract nature.

Yet, ironically, the shorter view Capitalocene, so rooted in the particular historical trajectory of British imperialism, is then extrapolated to become the universalised capital versus nature account of climate change. The British industrial capitalism around which Marx fashioned his model of the economy from his historical vantage point is retained as the model for all time, all space. The national contrasts between different capitalist economies, so clear in mid-nineteenth century, are deemed to evaporate under a presumed general model of growth. Other models of industrialisation in the twentieth century Soviet Union or contemporary China are brushed aside with a dismissive wave of the hand. The textile factory production, the prototypical capitalist and wage worker economic organisation, becomes the paradigm for a generic capitalism in relation again to a de-spatialised, de-qualitised nature.[3] The closed circuit formula, so widely invoked, the Money-Commodities-Money^{plus} circuit, becomes universalised: Money (capital to acquire means of production and pay workers' wages) induces the production of Commodities which when sold reward capitalists with more money than they started out with, Money^{plus}, in a never ending circuit of expansion. This characterisation of capitalist growth and

---

3 'Capitalist growth....is a set of relations just as much as a process, whose limitless expansion *advances by ordering humans and the rest of nature in abstract space and time* because that is where most surplus-value can be produced.' (Malm, 2016, Loc 6060).

the climate emergency falls to the temptation of counterposing a socioeconomic planetary concept, the Capitalocene, to the natural science Earth System concept of the Anthropocene. As will be discussed below, social science does not need to ape the natural sciences in making its complementary contributions.

THE METABOLIC RIFT

Marx himself did hint at an ecological Marxism in a few scattered comments which some writers have developed into a major account of capitalism in contradiction with nature. Marx called it the metabolic rift, and it is the third approach to be explored here. Its contemporary re-working provides a classic example of how something which Marx could and did know about is heralded as a truly extraordinary prescience of the twenty-first century socio-ecological crisis.[4]

In mid-nineteenth century Britain, there was an ecological crisis discussed and conceptualised by political economists and natural scientists alike. Interestingly, its primary empirical focus was on agriculture and the degradation of land. In dramatic terms, the exhaustion of the nutrient qualities of soil by intensive capitalist agriculture was described by the pioneer natural scientist, Justus von Liebig, as 'the robbery of nature'. Re-visiting the drama of guano discussed in the previous chapter, Liebig and other scientists had analysed the key naturally occurring chemicals ensuring the productivity of

---

4 'Marx's emphasis on the need to maintain the earth for the sake of "the chain of human generations".... captured the very essence of the present day notion of sustainable development.' (Foster, 2000, p. 164). Or again, 'In pinpointing the metabolic rift brought on by capitalist society they (Marx and Engels) captured the essence of the contemporary ecological problem.' (Foster, 2013, p. 12.).

soil, notably nitrogen and potassium. Liebig argued that with the intensive capitalist agriculture of Britain, these nutrient properties were being stripped from the soil. The result was declining agricultural productivity threatening economic growth and expansion. The response was twofold, on the one hand the import of guano on the massive scale outlined earlier, and on the other, the import of wheat, especially with the ending of corn tariffs, amounting to 25% of wheat consumption in Britain in mid-century. For gardeners accustomed to fertilising shrubs with bone meal, in 1837 on a slightly grander scale, Britain imported over £250,000 of human bones excavated from the battlefields of the Napoleonic war.

In the spirit of harmony between the natural science of soil chemistry and the science of political economy, the term metabolism refers to processes of material change in nature, plant and animal growth as a pertinent example. Marx referred to these as 'the universal metabolism of nature', processes that occurred both before and after the evolution of the human species. Within this universal natural metabolism, societies developed through a second, and mediating metabolism, the processes of change in the material nature of things by human labour, the social metabolism. In the course of human history, the social metabolism developed within the universal natural metabolism without significantly disrupting it – and, for Marx, could do so again under a socialist economy of cooperative agriculture.

But the ecological crisis of mid-nineteenth century agriculture exemplified the uniqueness of capitalism in disrupting this balance between the social and the universal nature metabolisms. The key quotation from Marx, oft recycled, contains the core concept of the metabolic rift:

> *...the entire spirit of capitalist production, which is oriented towards the most immediate monetary*

> *profit – stands in contradiction with agriculture,*
> *which has to concern itself with the whole gamut of*
> *permanent conditions of life required by the chain of*
> *human generations*
>
> (Marx, Capital, vol. 3,754).

It was not so much that nature proffered free gifts, but that capitalism attributed no value to the qualitative characteristics of natural metabolisms, only to the social metabolisms of human labour. The dominance of exchange values generated by labour to the exclusion of valuing what nature could do for humans created a historically unique and unprecedented rift between social metabolisms and the universal natural metabolisms.

The historical pathway to the development of the rift was directly related to the British agricultural ecological crisis. Through a succession of transformations, land became treated like any other kind of capital, as a resource for the extraction of profit and rent. In Britain, distinctively, the enclosure of the commons that had been an important self-subsistence resource for the peasantry led to the expulsion of large numbers of people from the countryside and the first agricultural revolution intensifying production. The capitalisation of land and the formation of an urban working class, in this account, went hand in hand. The subsequent emergence of industrial capitalism, and the development of an economy dominated by the division between the owners of the means of production and a wage earning proletariat consolidated a double metabolic rift: between town and country on the one hand, and the economic supremacy of labour-generated exchange value over the qualitative values of nature, on the other.

This double rift was further intensified by colonisation and the expropriation of lands in distant places. The metropolitan wage worker purchasing sugar and cotton clothing was both producing commodities for their capitalist employers and living off the produce of distant lands, including the produce of slavery. The earlier more intimate relations between food, land, life and human labour were broken asunder. As a peculiar twist to the connection between the agricultural ecological crisis and this wider and deeper rift of the social metabolism within the universal natural metabolism, both Marx and Engels referred to the waste of urban human excrement. Restoring the link between town and country, they advocated, would require the recycling of urban human excrement for fertilizing the land, reconnecting the social metabolism with the universal natural metabolism. In fact, many schemes to do so, including one by the social reformer Edwin Chadwick, foundered. For decades a dedicated fleet of ships transported London's human excrement and dumped it in the North Sea (Harvey, 2015, p. 30).

The concept of the metabolic rift, formed directly in relation to the specificities of the British mid-nineteenth century ecological crisis of agricultural productivity, has now been erected as a general paradigm for a globalised and homogeneous characterisation of the relation between capitalism and nature. By virtue of the fundamental rift and contradiction between labour-generated exchange values and the qualitative characteristics of natural processes, profit-seeking capital accumulation is in an inherently antagonistic relation to ecological sustainability.

> *The alienation from the earth is the* sine qua non *of the capitalist system.*
>
> (Foster, 2000, p. 174)

By advocating the metabolic rift as the foundation of an ecological Marxism, its proponents are arguing that the answers to the climate emergency are, in a fundamental sense, already there in Marx. The 'alienation from the earth' involves a global capitalist system on the one side and the planetary natural environment on the other. All ecological crises are the outcome of this fundamental contradiction. There is no specific climate change explanation: the metabolic rift is a generalisation from an ecological crisis to all environmental sustainability crises, including corporeal crises – threats to human health and biological well-being. The model of the capitalist economy, in particular the antagonistic relation between exchange values generated by abstract human labour and the qualitative characteristics derived from nature (use values), is taken for granted. Indeed, that antagonistic relation, the ascription to abstract human labour as the sole source of all market exchange values, was Marx's way of characterising the economy. As such, it was conceived first and foremost as a model of the economy, how the Money-Commodity-Money[plus] circuit underpins the accumulation of capital, the exploitation of labour, and the class divide between capitalists and wage-workers. As a conception of the economy, it was not primarily designed to be a theory of how an economy develops an antagonistic relation to nature. The metabolic rift is at most a consequential by-product, lurking in the margins of the overall theoretical framework. The alienation of the capitalist system from the earth is a conceptual artefact of a particular way of conceiving the economy. Moreover, it bears the political implication that the overthrow of capitalism is a *sine qua non* for saving the planet and preventing all other ecological disasters. We might not be able to wait that long.

UNEQUAL ECOLOGICAL EXCHANGE

Departing from some, but not all, major Marxist assumptions about capitalism, and hence of the relation between the economy and nature, the final conceptual framework to be considered here is that of unequal ecological exchange. To some extent, it picks up on one aspect of the metabolic rift discussed above, the exploitative relation between the metropolitan industrial centres and the environmentally resource-rich but economically less developed economies of the world. This, indeed, is the central focus of the unequal exchange, the pillaging of less powerful regions by the more powerful.

At root, this particular conception of unequal exchange rests on a very simple idea. Those with more money can exercise greater purchasing power over those with less money (Hornborg, 2016, p. 70), and thereby acquire energy (including labour energy) and environmental resources in order to generate yet more purchasing power. It is 'The Matthew Effect' writ large: to those with more, more shall be given. Or, to replace the Marxist conception of capitalism as a regime of labour exploitation as the sole source of generating profit (surplus value), the conception is simply the Money-Commodity-Money^{plus} circuit. In moralistic/political terms, it substitutes the evil of exploitation with money 'as the root of all evil' (Hornborg, 2016, p. 63). This does not mean that labour is not exploited, but it is exploited as a consequence only of the asymmetric exchange relation between those with more money (e.g. to pay wages, etc.) and those without money, unless in receipt of wages (Hornborg, 2014, p. 14).

This conception of the economy of money is immediately and inherently also an ecological concept: flows of money drive flows of energy. Energy is here understood in the broadest of terms, energy stored in raw materials as well as energy generated by labour. The implacable logic of the Money-Commodity-Money^{plus} circuit is thus to drive the exploitation of nature, without limits. At its most strident, money is accorded the historic role of generating the social relations of capitalism rather than being the medium of exchange through which those relations are made manifest in market prices (Hornborg, 2019, p. 76). So as the Money-Commodity-Money[plus] circuit expands, the global resources of energy, the space and time embodied in labour and its products, are re-arranged in such a way as to intensify unequal ecological exchanges. There is an ongoing vicious spiral of money and energy flow expansion, to the detriment of a sustainable planet.

> *General purpose money is intrinsically destructive of ecosystems.*
>
> (Hornborg, 2012, p. 4)

In this conception of the economy of capitalism, the technological transformations of the industrial revolution are interpreted as 'new and profitable systems for displacing work and environmental pressures to other populations and geographical areas' (Hornborg, 2016, p. 72). The technologies and exploitations of labour in the factories of the metropolis are founded on the asymmetric exchange of biophysical resources in the world market. In that sense, flows of money drive technological development, and asymmetric flows of global resources are what makes modern technologies possible. In a detailed analysis of flows of raw cotton and wheat, the trade between England and the US especially, are claimed to depend on the asymmetric exchange power of the metropolis with respect to the hinterlands (Hornborg, 2012, Chapter 5). The machines of the industrial revolution are the products of asymmetric global resource transfers (Hornborg, 2019, p. 80).

As with the preceding three conceptualisations of the relation between capitalism and nature, the unequal exchange conceptualisation is a singularly and generically global one. There are some particular limitations of this conceptualisation. The money begets more money circuits invoke a universal 'general purpose money', or an abstract money, M, as the root of all evil. In so doing, it seems to take 'the economy' out of social and political institutions. Yet, monies are historical and political institutions, and in recent histories, national political institutions, involving state power and legitimation. Not everyone can print or mint the money in general circulation, in Britain only the Royal Mint can. Convertability between currencies, along with terms of trade, whether in the mercantilist period of the eighteenth century, or in the free trade periods that succeeded it, are the consequences of political accords. It is unclear, theoretically or empirically, to what in the real world 'general purpose money' refers. Although slaves are mentioned as the labour embodied in the raw materials for the European metropolises, they were enslaved by acts of violence, not acquired by exchange, and even in the slave trade, Europeans acquired them in exchange for guns, textiles, shells or copper bars.

The asymmetries of exchange that are conceptually accorded such significance in driving ecological flows of energy of the industrial revolution are likewise abstracted from the succession of wars between European countries and a United States gaining its independence in its Revolutionary War. The acquisition of colonies and colonisation itself were not, in any meaningful sense, acts of exchange. When England acquired Dutch, French and Spanish colonies – so critical for its subsequent industrial supremacy – it was by acts of military force not purchasing power. Finally, with this universalist account of the power of money to drive asymmetric exchanges and energy flows there is no explanation of the specific exchanges that generate climate change, more a vision of indiscriminate or undifferentiated ecological destruction. There is no account of the why, how, where and when of the dynamic interaction between any given political economy and nature that generated an unprecedented transformation of the earth's atmosphere.

All four of these conceptualisations of the relation between capitalism and nature grasp, to a greater or lesser degree, the critical historical importance of industrial capitalism for the environmental sustainability of human and non-human life on the planet. The shorter view Capitalocene concept is the only one to explore a direct dynamic between industrial capitalism, steam power and climate change. The longer view Capitalocene, rightly, insists on the preceding scale of environmental impacts, especially land-use change arising from European colonisation, plantation economies and expanding commodity frontiers, but without directly addressing their relative significance for climate change. Yet all are ultimately constrained by an adherence to some principles of a generic capitalist economy abstracted from either their socio-political or more importantly from their environmental resource contexts. The Capitalocene, both versions, adhere to a foundation concept of the generation of profits from abstract labour time, and all adhere to some version of the Money-Commodity-Money[plus] circuit. Finally, all are characterised by a version of the self-destruction concept of the second contradiction: capitalism destroys itself by destroying the environmental and biological conditions of its own reproduction. Whether it is the end of the four cheaps, the declining rate of profit, or simply extreme environmental events, capitalism's relation to nature is ultimately unsustainable. These conceptualisations of capitalism implicitly carry the daunting consequence that as long as the fundamental logics of the abstract capitalist economy are in place, the earth system is doomed.

The concept of sociogenesis fully embraces the significance of the long emergence of industrial capitalism as a decisive historical period for climate change. But its view of the economy and capitalism breaks from the limitations rooted in nineteenth century thinking, and the historical materialism predicated on a particular conceptualisation of the economy of capitalism. Sociogenesis characterises capitalist political economies as more like a hydra-headed monster, with each of its heads splitting away with varying political directions and inhabiting different environmental contexts, rather than endowed with a generic and implacable logic of a machine. Moreover, the concept of sociogenesis is not limited to the analysis of hydra-headed capitalisms.

The sociogenesis concept is broad enough to analyse the historical and spatial variety of different societal economies in their environmental contexts, from the earliest epochs of domestication of crops and animals through to twentieth and twenty-first-century processes of industrialisation. The intensive industrialisation of the Soviet bloc, and its industrial legacies, are of a major significance in generating climate change and will be addressed further below. Just to note here, Lenin famously pronounced: 'Communism is Soviet power plus the electrification of the whole country, since industry cannot be developed without electrification'. The very first Soviet economic plan was dedicated to electrification by means of combining coal-fired power stations with hydro-electric power. However one classifies the long development of China's economy under Mao Tse-Tung, and then market socialism, it has been a politically directed economy, now the second largest and soon to become the largest. It makes no sense to analyse its distinctive significance for climate change in terms of an ecologically re-heated nineteenth century model of capitalism (see Chapters 4 and 5).

What difference does a sociogenesis concept of capitalism make for understanding climate change? The importance of the factory system of cotton textile production has figured prominently in both the natural science and social science already discussed. In the next chapter, more empirical substance will be offered, while here the conceptual gain of sociogenesis is highlighted by picking this one example. The sociogenesis approach analyses different configurations going from production through to consumption, taking in different forms of exchange and appropriation, and how goods and people are spatially distributed. As a quick summary, these are production-distribution-exchange-consumption configurations or, to give it an acronym, PDEC configurations (Harvey, 2007). So, in mid-nineteenth century raw cotton was produced in the Deep South of the United States by 3 million slaves, with 80% of the crop going to the Lancashire cotton mills. There was a mixture of appropriation by violence and markets for slaves and cotton. Plantations were modern, finance capital supported, profit-making economies of production. From a climate change perspective, they were a significant aspect of a massive land-use change with expanding populations displacing native Americans by ethnic cleansing and genocides. Deforestation and land cultivation released greenhouse gases. Then, supported by British banks providing credit, the cotton went to the Liverpool cotton exchange, to be distributed to the cotton mills. The cotton mills are prototypical of the emergent industrial proletariat and wage labour, with an industrial workforce of 460,000 to complement the 3 million slaves in mid-century. Processes of qualitative transformation of the raw cotton, spinning, weaving, dying, printing, resulted in a qualitatively novel range of fabrics. Cotton textiles displaced woollen, linen and leather previously produced domestically. A significant proportion of these textiles were exported to Europe and the rest of the world. The whole pattern of clothing consumption, wear and care was transformed, including cotton textiles purchased by wage labourers working across industries in Great Britain. For climate change, the significance, already highlighted, is of clothing produced by means of steam power, using a distinctive coal resource found within Britain in reasonable spatial proximity to the factory systems (Harvey, 2019).

This cotton textile PDEC configuration sociogenically induced climate change both in the Deep South of the United States and in the factories of Lancashire, and did so only in its distinctive combination. As a system of production of both raw materials and finished textiles it relied on the transformation of clothing, with qualitative distinctions generating demand by consumers, rich and poor. This emphasis on production for consumption is important not only because of a totally new dimension to the quality of clothing, but because inequalities in consumption and hence inequalities in the generation of climate change according to income, are a significant focus of current debates. In the four Marxist conceptualisations analysed earlier, consumption scarcely figures, let alone inequalities of consumption. Sociogenically, it was only as a combination of land-use change and fossil fuel energy for steam-powered machinery that the PDEC configuration induced climate change. The coal would not have been burnt for that purpose without the land-use change for its purpose, and vice versa. In terms of exchange and appropriation, it was a combination of market exchanges for wage labour and the force and violence of slavery, not one or the other. In terms of distribution, it was the combination of movements of slaves from the Old South to the Deep South, and cotton transported from the Deep South to Lancashire, followed by textiles across the United Kingdom and exports across Europe and the wider world.

At this slice in time, mid-nineteenth century, this was a distinctively British-US Deep South configuration, a hybrid hydra-head, joining finance capital with profits from slavery generated quite differently from profits from wage labour under the British Master and Servants Acts. This was no abstract model capitalism going worldwide generating that sharp acceleration of greenhouse gas emissions. Nor did this cotton PDEC characterise the whole of the British economy or its peculiar industrial revolution. It was terminated, moreover, not by economic competition or pressure, but by Civil War in the United States – with slavery to be replaced in large measure only by other forms of servitude – and by changes in labour law in the United Kingdom. It was a climate-changing PDEC configuration that had its time and place.

Key to this sociogenic conceptualisation of capitalism for accounting for climate change is to view labour – in any societal economic organisation and under whatever labour regimes – as a process of qualitative transformations of qualitative natural properties. It matters how and where labour changes land use, clears forests or savannahs, temperate or tropical. It matters that coal has qualitative characteristics that can then be transformed by varied processes of mining and burning, and how fossil fuel energy is then used to power machinery or generate electricity. And finally, quality transformations create new markets, with quality distinctions and differentiations, and consequentially command, in the asymmetric power relations between producers, retailers and consumers, the prices that consumers eventually pay. Cotton textiles in all their variety created new markets, and displaced others – and continue to do so to this day, with other forms of exploitative labour in global supply chains. It should never be forgotten that where labour creates quality distinctions consumers end up paying the price of profits.

In this sense, a Marxist conceptualisation of profit under capitalism as derived from the abstract labour time involved in producing any commodity (including labour itself) directly obstructs analysis of how labour through its qualitative transformations, generates climate change. Quantities of abstract labour time as such do not generate greenhouse gases, whereas different qualitative labour processes do, and in different ways. But Marx's model of a capitalist economy was not designed to analyse the particular interactions between economies and resource environments that generate climate change. That is its limitation, and adherence to its principles continue to constrain the four conceptualisations discussed above. It was a model that excluded such an analysis. As we have seen, Marxists attribute to the reality of industrial capitalism that externalisation of Nature. Capitalism is a motor that develops in disregard or denial of Nature, hence its destructiveness. But that disregard is just as much a characteristic of Marx's model, preventing conceptualisation of precisely those interactions that are the defining characteristic of industrial capitalism: the agricultural revolutions, the burning of coal, the deforestations. Marx didn't – couldn't – know that clearing and deep tilling land released CO_2, or that coal did likewise. For those that critique dualism, Marx's theory of capitalism enshrined a dualism at its core between the products of human labour on the one side and on the other side, natural gifts, all that is produced naturally, through biology, solar radiation, fossilisation. It is Marx that logically abstracts the market economy from nature, so necessarily placing it in an alienating and destructive relation to nature. The theory was developed in order to account for relative prices of market goods, for the difference between the value created by labour in production for the market and the value of labour, when worker sells their labour. It was a theory of the economy, not of the dynamic relations between economies and their natural environments. As a consequence, everything that is not produced by labour, and by quantities of it measured by time, lies outside the exchange value economy. It is not a theory of the dualism of capitalism, but a dualistic theory of capitalism. Nature becomes abstract nature as a by-product of treating all qualitative differences of matter as of no significance for market prices and exchange, once transformed by labour into a marketable commodity, where only the abstract labour embodied in it counts for price.

Sociogenesis of climate change thus entails a radically different way of thinking about capitalist economies – with all their historically divergent hydra-heads and environmental contexts – placing qualitative transformations of natural processes at the core. This is what constitutes a historical materialism fit for the twenty-first century, appropriate to address the climate emergency. How and where fossil fuels are developed, produced and consumed; how and where changes in land use occur and to what use (food, energy); these are the historically material qualitative transformations that matter. As represented in Fig. 1.2, economies are placed in the resource environments over which they have command, and in which they historically evolve.

Finally, as also represented in Fig. 1.2, economies do not have an implacable logic outside of the political processes that institute them: laws of property, employment laws, slavery laws, company laws, fiscal and tax laws, contract and trading laws, and so on. Political processes set the rules of the economic games, and vary, nation to nation, historical period to historical period. Profits made in Manchester or New Orleans in the mid-nineteenth century are not made the same way that Amazon makes its profits in the twenty-first century. The significance of the eighteenth century European wars has already been alluded to for any understanding of why, where and how the industrial revolution occurred. However frequent are the wars of economic competition between states, states can also exercise softer powers in promoting their economic competitive advantage. Across these many dimensions, economies are politically instituted, and so open to political de- and re-institution. If the pandemic has shown nothing else, it has shown, and in peacetime, the power of the state to reshape and command an economy, as did the politics of austerity, debt bail-outs, banking regulation and reform, following the 2007–2008 financial crisis. Abstract models of the economy de-politicise and reify the logics and inequalities of contemporary capitalist economies. When considering the politics of climate change and the economic transformations necessary to avoid a climate catastrophe, we do not have the luxury to wait for or precipitate the collapse of capitalism and its abstract logics of environmental self-destruction.

3

HISTORICAL PATHWAYS TO CLIMATE CHANGE

When it comes to climate change, the past is present. As natural scientists have demonstrated, the increase of greenhouse gases (GHG) in the atmosphere is cumulative through human history unless active measures are taken to reduce it, for example through the creation of carbon sinks, reforestation or algae farms. For an analysis of the already changed climate, the concept of sociogenesis must therefore turn to history, and, in turn, history must be re-written through the lens of climate change.

There is no ambition here to provide a world history, and in any case, it is not clear what such a history might deliver. Instead, the approach in the following chapters is to take some specific historical pathways to climate change of particular societies at times of significant transition. The aim of this approach is to advance understanding of the political, economic and social processes involved in sociogenic climate change. In this chapter two contrasting pathways provide the principal examples: the British industrial revolution together with the early nineteenth century slave plantation, and an example of settler colonialism in the United States. Neither of these historical pathways have been written through the lens of climate change, although there is a vast historical literature of both these transformatory processes. By focusing the climate change lens on these pathways, the schematic accounts that follow are necessarily partial, covering neither the British industrial revolution as a whole nor the expansion Southwards and Westwards entailed in the enlargement of the United States. Whereas coal will figure in the case of the British industrial revolution, cattle will form an important element of the United States pathway. Slave plantations are the bridging link between these two pathways. And just to note here that the particular significance of cattle in the United States story is only a distinctive but representative example of a major and yet little heralded phenomenon of huge climate change significance: the introduction of cattle from Europe and India into the Americas as a new and invasive species (Bowling, 1942; Ficek, 2019). Cumulatively, it was a multi-million 'cattle drive' of truly gigantic proportions, all animals emitting methane.

In the first chapter, it was argued that the concept of sociogenesis was complementary to, rather than contesting or replacing, the natural science understanding of the anthropogenesis of climate change. There is a need to weld together the societal dynamics of climate change with the environmental dynamics. This approach underpins the analysis of the two historical pathways, and subsequent chapters, by asking particular questions of the historical and contemporary pathways to climate change. Below is a diagram which serves as a tool-kit for asking these questions. In environmental science, the diagram represents what has been called the food-energy-climate change trilemma (Tilman et al., 2009). The diagram thus pictures the natural science bare bones to which the sociogenesis approach will add the historical and social flesh.

Taking a walk through the diagram, we follow the arrows using contemporary examples from research into today's food-energy-climate change trilemma (Harvey, 2014; Harvey & Pilgrim, 2011). The arrows 1 and 2 represent the main sources of greenhouse gases driving climate change, the burning of fossil fuels for various types of energy and the use and changes in use of land for food, energy, and materials. Increased demand for energy for transport, and power generation for industrial and domestic uses directly drives the increased generation of GHG from fossil fuels (arrow 3). Likewise, increased and changing demand for food, increased consumption of meat, nutrition and growing populations directly drives the intensification of land use *and* land-use change converting uncultivated land (e.g. forests, savannahs) into agricultural land (arrow 4) (see Fig. 3.1).

This directly increases the generation of a variety of greenhouse gases from land use and changes in use. Both

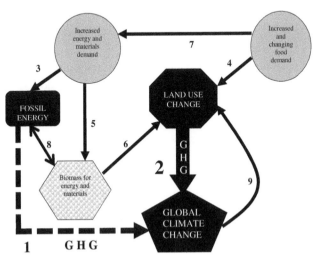

Fig. 3.1. The Natural Science Food-energy-climate Change Trilemma.

historically, and today, demand for energy has not only relied on fossil fuels, but also on wood (including charcoal), and, on its way to fossilisation, peat. And in addition to energy, raw materials for building, clothing, etc. further increase demand for the products of land (biomass), (arrow 5). In turn these increased demands for biomass intensify and compete with demands on land for food (arrow 6), so adding to the GHG generated from land (back to arrow 2). Agricultural use of land in itself is a significant source of increased demand for energy, through use of machinery consuming fossil fuels and, in the contemporary world, the use of chemical fertilizers. Transport of food across the globe, especially counter-seasonal food, much of it airlifted, adds a further major demand for fossil energy (arrow 7). All this therefore adds to the generation of greenhouse gases from fossil fuels (back to arrow 1). Whether in the eighteenth and nineteenth centuries or today, there is a competition or tension between the alternatives of using fossil energy, such as coal, or biomass energy, such as wood. Depending on shifts in use between fossil or renewable biomass, further pressures are added either to fossil fuel consumption or to demand for land (arrow 8). More about that immediately follows. Finally, climate change bites back, particularly in the form of droughts, floods, and other extreme weather events, but also in the slower but equally significant changes that affect what can be cultivated where. The climate change induced spread of novel animal pests in Africa are an early warning of further impacts of climate change on food production. All these changes form a feed-back loop intensifying pressures on the use of land and land-use change (arrow 9).

In the contemporary world, the trilemma has taken a particular shape in particular countries. Moreover, the trilemma is a very twenty-first century way of looking at the challenges of climate change. It is an analytical lens born of the present but instrumental in rewriting the past. In doing so, it is imperative to grasp the difference of the past from the present. Present trilemmas are not just repetitions of past trilemmas. How one understands the present makes a difference to how one understands the past – and vice versa. So before delving into the two main historical pathways, here is the briefest of sketches of Brazil's current trilemma, to hold in mind in order to appreciate how different it is from the trilemmas of the early nineteenth century of industrial capitalism and settler colonisation. It fleshes out the sociogenic dynamics so qualitatively distinctive of Brazil.

In terms of the two main trilemma drivers of climate change, use of fossil energy and land use, Brazil stands out in contrast to any other country in the world. It has by far the largest proportion of renewable energy production and use of any country, let alone developed economies. A combination of a significant level of hydroelectric power for power generation and a world-leading percentage of renewable fuel for its transport fleet results in 42% of its total energy being renewable. The United Kingdom, after a period of considerable development of wind and solar power and limited adoption of a biofuel mix reaches a total of 12% for overall energy use. The United States, in spite of being the largest producer of biofuels to mix with fossil fuels, reaches a total of only 7%, including its development of solar and wind power. Most strikingly, Brazil has a unique domestic car fleet of Flex-Fuel Vehicles that allows the consumer to switch from bioethanol to petrol at the fuel pump stations, according to relative prices. In 2018 there were 27 million Flex-Fuel Vehicles, reaching 73% of the total fleet. This is a distinctively Brazilian phenomenon, driven by long term political strategies. President Lula promoted these vehicles, negotiating with the major car manufacturers to produce a dedicated Brazilian fleet. It follows a much longer scientific, economic and national self-interest policy supporting its sugar cane industry going back to the 1930s. This state strategy was in part also stimulated by the oil-price shocks of the 1970s which made oil-importing developing countries extremely vulnerable and dollar-dependent. Now Brazil is 100% energy self-sufficient, even exceeding the United States after its fracking boom had secured a 92% energy self-sufficiency rising from 70% a decade ago. Germany, by contrast, is only 33% self-sufficient in energy (International Energy Agency, Energy Atlas, 2020). In terms of energy, Brazil demonstrates how a particular political economy, driven by strategic developmental objectives, interacts with its distinctive land resource environment to generate hydroelectric power and sugarcane bioethanol.

That is the relatively benign energy horn of Brazil's trilemma. But its very positivity intensifies its land-use pressures on climate change. Whether for hydroelectric power and dam construction or the expansion of land under sugarcane agriculture, the impacts on land use and land use change have been the subject of enormous controversy over the decades. At the heart of the controversy lies the pushing ever-outwards of the commodity frontiers, converting non-agricultural land – the Amazon tropical rain forest and Mato Grasso savannah biomes in particular – into agricultural land. Sugarcane itself is only one element in this dynamic. As we shall see in the following chapter, both the humble soya bean and cattle play a far greater role. But all, directly or indirectly, increase demand for land, and whether from land use change, or from agricultural processes of land use themselves, the consequence is a significant increase in greenhouse gases. Iconically, the deforestation of the Amazon has been the focus of global attention both for its significance for climate change, and for the loss of biological species. Until the election of Bolsonaro in January 2019, strict state regulation and satellite monitoring as well as corporate moratoria had succeeded in reducing, but far from eliminating, the deforestation of the Amazon. As a consequence of previous extensification of agricultural activity and logging, a huge pool of degraded pastureland had been created, available for more productive agriculture. Yet, the same developmental policies that had driven Brazil's energy economy had resulted in Brazil becoming the agricultural powerhouse of the world. Brazil is now the largest exporter of beef, poultry, coffee, orange juice, and, overtaking the USA, soya. Brazil's agricultural land has been increasing by five million hectares every year since the 1990s. It has a cattle herd of over 200 million. To make the point, Brazil has been able to develop in this way because it has the land, sun, and water resources to do so. That is its particular – sociogenic – trilemma characteristic.

Land use and land use change are Brazil's primary sociogenic drivers of climate change, not fossil energy consumption. The consequence for climate change and climate change mitigation are equally distinctive for Brazil as food producer and consumer, as we shall see further in the following chapter. But it means that Brazil has a quite distinctive greenhouse signature. Over 60% of its total greenhouse gas emissions come from land use, peat destruction and deforestation, outweighing all emissions from buildings, infrastructure and industry. For the USA – itself not an insignificant agricultural economy – greenhouse gas emissions from its land use and land use change only account for less than 10% of its total emissions, a proportion only slightly exceeded by the European Union 27 countries, averaging 12% (UNDP, 2012).

Enter Bolsonaro, elected President of Brazil in January 2019. A climate change denier, he has proclaimed a policy of commercialisation of the Amazon and relaxed controls over the incursion of agriculture and logging into the region. Dramatic recordings of the Amazon on fire appeared across the globe. Over 10,000 square kilometres of deforestation have intensified Brazil's distinctive global climate change drivers to the extreme. The political direction of Brazil's economic development has taken a turn, amplifying the climate emergency within its special environmental context. Not all nations have the Amazon or the Mato Grasso savannah in their back gardens.

Hold this cameo of a twenty-first-century Brazilian sociogenic trilemma in mind, and now plunge back into history and the first great acceleration of sociogenic climate change. Then too, in the two pathways we are about to analyse, there were the key components of the trilemma: fossil or pre-fossil energy from coal or peat versus renewable energy from wood and charcoal; and food and clothing transitions as drivers for the expansion and intensification of agricultural land use and land use change. The qualitative contrasts between past and present trilemmas, different political economies in interaction with different resource environments at different historical times, are at the heart of a sociogenic understanding of climate change. Complementary to the natural scientific anthropogenic accounts, but engaging with the particular dynamics inducing climate change, contemporary and historical, the sociogenic concept goes beyond the globalist and abstract capitalist perspective as discussed in the previous chapter. Contemporary trilemma thinking makes it possible to interrogate the past of climate change in a more powerful and novel way.

Thus historians of the industrial revolution and United States expanding colonisation have woven together powerful narratives of the economies of energy, clothing, wages, food, timber, land, whole histories of development and economic transformation. They have done so without the slightest nod or acknowledgement of their significance for climate change. Such narratives need rewriting.

A useful starting point for understanding the sociogenic trilemma driving the British industrial revolution pathway to economic dominance and inequalities between nations is counting sheep. Much has been written about the importance of the agricultural revolution and enclosures in the seventeenth and eighteenth centuries as the necessary precondition for Britain's subsequent industrial take-off. The woollen industry had already been significant before a period of very rapid growth during the eighteenth century. The number of sheep increased massively from around eight million in 1700 to over 16 million by the early nineteenth century (Turner, 1998). At that point, sheep outnumbered cattle by roughly seven times, and humans in the whole of Great Britain by 50% (according to the first census of 1801). This was not just a numerical growth, as new breeds with longer and finer fleeces, notably the Leicester breeds, spread through England, especially in the North East. The growing production of the finer worsted textiles established England as the premier woollen textile manufacturer in Europe. In the course of a century, by the 1770s, woollen exports had nearly tripled and accounted for over 40% of British exports, predominantly to Europe, followed by the Americas (Harley, 2004).

From the English sociogenic trilemma perspective, sheep have a lot of ramifications. At its most direct, 16 million sheep emit a lot of methane, and a back of the envelope calculation would suggest that they produced in the region of 38.3 million tons of CO_2eq. per year. By 1800, this would have been a significant proportion of England's total greenhouse gas emissions. This perspective also supports the general line of argument for the environmental science Long View of climate change. It strongly points to the presence of higher and growing levels of emissions *prior* to the take-off of steam power and coal energy consumption.

The growth in numbers of sheep also inevitably reflected a change in demand for land and type of land use, with millions of acres of land, including high quality land, being converted from arable to pasture as a consequence in part of depopulation following the Black Death. Sheep benefitted from access to higher quality land, with the average carcass weight tripling by 1800, and the weight of the fleece more than doubling (Allen, 2009). In general, the more carcass weight reflects more vegetation conversion, and hence more methane per sheep.

The growth in numbers of sheep and land-use are directly central to the early stages of development of the British industrial revolution climate change trilemma. But the indirect effects are perhaps equally significant, notably the growth in urban and particularly London's population, and the proto-industrialisation that created a platform for subsequent full-blown industrialisation. These indirect effects are necessarily less tangible, let alone quantifiable. But that does not diminish their importance.

The growth of the woollen trade was particularly important for London as the principal trading entrepot. Even before the beginning of the eighteenth century, woollen textiles contributed to three quarters of its export trade, and a quarter of London's workforce was engaged in export trading. The growth of London, in comparison with any other European urban centre was dramatic, becoming the largest city in Europe. From 1700 to 1800 it grew from 575,000 to 865,000, with 70% of urban growth in the whole of Europe being concentrated in England (Wrigley, 2000). Woollen textiles were a major contributor to that growth.

More significant for climate change than simple numerical urban growth, however, was the leading role of London in bringing about the distinctive English shift to burning coal as the main fuel for domestic heating. The growth in population entailed building houses on an unprecedented scale, but, more importantly a radical and complex innovation in how consumers heated their homes. Burning coal required a complete redesign of the fire place itself (e.g. iron grates), and different chimneys to accelerate the flow of oxygen through the fuel. London led the way in building design, particularly following the Great Fire of 1666. The consumption of coal – the coal revolution – was dramatic and unparalleled in the rest of Europe. From 227,000 tons in 1560, it rose to nearly 2 million tons in 1700, only to accelerate to a total of 15 million tons by 1800. The revolution was not only an aspect of the consumption end of house design and heating. The coal revolution reflected the central trilemma tension of land versus energy. By 1800, burning coal in England was producing the equivalent energy of 15 million acres of woodland. Yet, in 1800 England only had 1.25 million acres of woodland available for fuel (Allen, 2009). The shift from a renewable fuel (wood and charcoal) to a fossil fuel was 'the European way of saving land' (Malanima, 2006, p. 120). It was an escape from the finite resources of the surface environment.

In fact, it was distinctively the British way of saving land. The shift to coal, from the production end, was reflected in the rocketing costs of charcoal and wood, compared with coal. Per unit of heat, in London as the centre of the domestic coal revolution, the real costs of coal remained static through the late seventeenth and eighteenth centuries, while the costs of wood/charcoal quadrupled, becoming three times the costs of coal. The coal flowed at low cost from Newcastle to the capital. This was the English economy's distinctive resource environment (Fig. 1.2), already manifest before the take-off of the industrial revolution. Simplifying a complex picture of European energy resources, perhaps the most striking contrast was between England and its closest economic rival of the seventeenth and eighteenth century, the Dutch Republic.

Although it too could have imported coals from Newcastle, the Dutch Republic was sitting on vast reserves of peat, its principal energy resource. It was not until the nineteenth century, when costs of peat and of redesigning houses and industry changed the equations, that the Dutch made the switch from native peat to imported coal. By then, the British sociogenic climate change pathway – and its industrial revolution – had put Britain in a different league.

So, returning to the trilemma diagram and following the arrows: expansion of sheep numbers and quality ↔ changing land use and the expansion of the woollen trade ↔ urbanisation and new house building and design ↔ the switch and dramatic growth of coal consumption. Although indirect, these two-way arrows represent the dynamic interconnection between methane from sheep, changes in land-use, and CO_2 from domestic burning of fossil energy. This is not to suggest any direct or one-way causal link between sheep and coal, let alone to weigh down sheep with the full burden of explanation. There were multiple, interacting dimensions to the historical transformations in this pre-industrial revolution period. But, for certain, sheep and domestic coal consumption were well in the mix.

The proto-industrial developments of woollen textile production and consumption were the second principal but indirect ramification of sheep for Britain's climate change pathway. Through the course of the eighteenth century, woollen production and in particular the development of the new draperies resulted in the transformation of the industry. Increasingly, the use of water power replaced human energy in weaving and spinning yarn. Technologies of water mills were pioneered in wool, before the rapid growth of the cotton industry. The West Riding of Yorkshire became the hub of the new industries. Moreover, the development of skills in woollen textile production were readily transferrable into the cotton textile industries, providing a knowledge platform for the subsequent transformational growth of cotton textiles (Mokyr, Sarid, & van der Beek, 2019).

To a certain degree, then, contrary to their reputation, sheep led the way into the industrial revolution and all else followed them. But it did not stop there. Although, as we shall shortly see, cotton manufacture has been seen as the miracle industry of the industrial revolution, woollen textile production continued to flourish in the nineteenth century. Technical innovations in spinning wool yarn and mechanical shuttle weaving were complemented by the adoption of cotton as the warp for light worsted textiles, with wool as the weft. Steam power and factory-based machine-driven weaving, radically reduced the proto-industrial significance of hand-loom production. In 1836, there were already 2,768 power looms in the West Riding, but within just over two decades, the number had increased tenfold, to 29,539 in 1850. Woollen textile production transitioned from proto- to a full blown industrial-revolutionary feature of the economy, reliant on fossil fuel energy (Hudson, 2002). Methane from sheep was now *directly* conjoined with CO_2 from coal, as the adoption of coal for mechanical energy overtook the consumption of coal for domestic heating. The proto-industrialisation with the switch to coal as a primary source of domestic heating energy, created a uniquely British platform for an industrial revolution and climate change pathway, with coal now as a major source of mechanical energy.

Moreover, in terms of consumption, although undoubtedly cotton textiles became dominant during the early nineteenth century, they were additions rather than replacements to the wardrobe, introducing new ranges and seasonalities to what consumers wore. Factory-produced worsteds complemented cotton textiles, and woollen clothing continued to command significant consumer markets particularly in temperate and northern climates (Hudson, 2008). Bradford, as the 'wor-stedopolis' of Yorkshire, could boast that its worsteds were produced at a price competitive with cotton textiles, and widely worn by working and middle class English men and women. They had a premier place in that celebration of the British industrial revolution, the Great Exhibition of 1851 (Sigsworth, 1952).

Sheep, land use and domestic energy coal gave a distinctive initial twist to the British climate change pathway. Cotton, land use and mechanical energy coal represented a massive step change in the same direction of travel. As discussed above and in the previous chapter, cotton textile manufacture led the way in the switch from water power to steam power to drive the machinery of textile manufacture. Moreover, just as coal for domestic heating represented a distinctively English development in overcoming the trilemma pressure on demand for land for wood as a source of fuel, so coal for mechanical energy did likewise. When considering the cotton textile trajectory, therefore, there is on the one hand land saving in England from coal, and on the other, land gaining through the expansion of cotton plantation economies first in the Caribbean and then in the American Deep South. Each had a climate change significance in their own right, but only together did they define the distinctively British sociogenic pathway.

So turning to coal first, England led the world in the production and consumption of coal for a whole range of its uses, initially but continuously domestic heating, and iron production, then steam-powered machinery, across industry and transport (railways, iron-clad shipping).

> *Britain was first because Britain had coal – a fact of nature, not an artefact of history.*
>
> (Allen, 2009, p. 81)

Cotton textile production in factories spearheaded steam power manufacturing, exploiting an immediate resource environment advantage, the development of coal mining in Lancashire in closeness, proximity to the import of cotton via Liverpool and the centres of production. This exemplified a particular interaction between a political economy and its resource environment. Although it is not possible to apportion the precise percentage of mechanical energy coal to cotton textile production as opposed to other industrial uses, there can be no doubt of its dominance in the burning of fossil fuel. From an already rapidly expanding production of cotton textiles in the pre-steam power era, between 1800 and 1850 the volume of cotton manufacture increased 10 times, reaching 370,000 tons by that time. The number of spindles grew from seven million in 1820 to 21 million by 1850. By 1835 there were 1,500 factory manufacturers, rising to 4,000 by 1860 (Beckert, 2015). The parallel increase in coal consumption from 1800 to 1855 was from 11 million tons to 65 million tons. By comparison, the total coal consumption of the next three biggest coal nations, Belgium, France and Germany combined was 18.6 million tons, and their combined cotton textile production was less than one third of the British industry. In per capita terms, the contrast in coal consumption between its combined continental rivals and Britain was even greater: 0.24 tons per person each year as against 2.87 tons per person per year (Wrigley, 2013). Even restricting the analysis to coal, the switch from an organic energy economy to a fossil energy economy resulted in the unique sociogenic British pathway to climate change, contributing over twice as much CO_2 in 1850 as those three continental rivals combined. Given the contemporary renewable energy alternatives and their dependence on extensive land, simply put, there would have been no industrial revolution without a major impact on climate change.

> *The move away from an exclusively organic*
> *economy was a* sine qua non *of achieving a capacity*
> *for exponential growth.*
>
>   (Wrigley, 2000, p. 139)

But burning coal for steam powered manufacturing only occurred in conjunction with raw materials, notably cotton. Cotton, moreover, represents a major dimension of 'the great divergence' in relation to the second main driver of climate change: land use, and land use change. England in particular broke out of the confines of its own national territorial agricultural land by colonial expansion, and later by its command over slave plantations in the US Deep South. The principal technological innovations in cotton manufacture (Hargreave's spinning jenny, 1764; Arkwright's water frame, 1769; Crompton's mule, 1779) coincided with the switch from London and the Orient to Liverpool and slave plantations in Brazil and the Caribbean as ports of entry and sources of cotton respectively. Thereafter, following the American Revolutionary War in 1783, the growth in imports was dominated by the United States, with over 50% of all cotton imports coming from there already by 1815.

The development of slave cotton in the USA was driven by the British cotton textile industry. Through its credit financing of cotton crops, purchasing of slaves and land, Britain obtained dominant control of the expansion of cotton production in the US Deep South. By 1850, England purchased over 70% of the total United States cotton crop, and the number of cotton slaves had increased from nearly 900,000 in 1820 to three million by that time. Conversely, the dependence of the British cotton textile industry was even greater. By 1860, 88 per cent of the textiles produced by British factories were made with US slave cotton (Harvey, 2019). Such was the intimate relation between British cotton manufacturing and slave cotton from the United States that an editorial of the *London Times* in 1857 suggested that economically England was in effect a constituent state of the United States.

> *We know that for all mercantile purposes England is one of the States, and that, in effect, we are partners with the southern planter; we hold a bill of sale over his goods and chattels, his live and dead stock, and take a lion's share in the profits of slavery…We are clothing not only ourselves, but all the world besides, with the very cotton picked by 'Uncle Tom' and his fellow-sufferers. It is our trade. It is the great staple of British industry.*

The history of cotton slavery, and British involvement with it, has been written overwhelmingly in terms of the great divergence in economic development. Along with its own sugar slave Caribbean plantation economies, Britain became the dominant imperial and economic capitalist power by the middle of the nineteenth century. But by virtue of its control, whether political or economic, over huge new land resources in the New World, this economic development was equally significant for climate change. The expansion of its distinctive capitalist agricultural resources was dynamically tied to the conversion and subsequent exploitation of huge tracts of land. In terms of the trilemma this expansion of land resources in the United States was intrinsically related to its consumption of domestic fossil energy, the twin drivers of climate change. This was at the core of the British sociogenic trilemma of its major industrial revolution manufacturing capacity.

Let us pause for a moment to recall the environmental science Long View of climate change. The slow development and spread of domesticated crops and animals, beginning with rice cultivation, made a significant if gradual contribution over many centuries to anthropogenic climate change prior to

the rapid acceleration induced by fossil fuels from industrialisation in the early nineteenth century. By comparison, in the
course of a few decades the whole continent of North America
and much of South America witnessed land conversion of a
much more intensive nature. Cotton was a central element of
that conversion, although, as we shall see, only part of a
bigger picture when we come to consider the distinctive United
States sociogenic pathway.

Land conversion in the United States was predominantly
not the relatively innocent taming of wild nature, but the
expropriation of Native American lands by successive genocides and ethnic cleansings. It was the brutal replacement of
settled subsistence agricultures or hunter-gatherer societies by
commercial agriculture on a massive spatial scale, and in
climate change terms, over a very short period of time. An
historical landmark in this process was the so-called Louisiana
Purchase of 1803, when the United States, with the aid of the
British bank Barings, acquired from the French an amount of
land that *doubled* the then size of the United States. For the
price of $15 million, the United States bought 2.1 million
square kilometres, an area which covers Louisiana itself,
Arkansas, Missouri, Iowa, Minnesota, Montana, Oklahoma,
Kansas, Nebraska, North and South Dakota, and parts of
Wyoming and Colorado. This is not usually heralded as a
climate change event, but it was, especially given President
Jefferson's ambition to either civilise Native Americans into
modern agriculturists or displace and exterminate them.

In a sense, the Louisiana Purchase was the acquisition of
nominal political control as the precondition for the
advancement of the settler and planter colonisation of the new
territory. Already in existing states, wars against Native
American Nations had opened the ground for slave plantations, including those dedicated to cotton production. Even by
1800, 416,018 acres were dedicated to growing cotton for

England alone (Beckert, 2015). Following the defeat at the battle of Horseshoe Bend in 1814 the Creeks ceded 23 million hectares for future plantation agriculture in Georgia and Alabama under the Treaty of Fort Jackson. The 1819 Treaty with the Choctaw Nation, again militarily enforced by Andrew Jackson, ceded a further five million hectares in the key Yazoo-Mississippi Delta for cotton cultivation. By the end of the 1830s, Mississippi produced more cotton than any other Southern State, and together with the Louisiana Purchase states of Louisiana itself, Alabama, and Arkansas accounted for over 70% of the total area under cotton cultivation.

Although far more significant as crimes against humanity, from a climate change perspective the genocidal wars cleared the land for slavery plantations. This was the first phase of relatively high levels of greenhouse gas emissions arising from the rapid conversion of largely uncultivated land into intensive farming. Involving a range of biomes, it would be hard to calculate the impact on the atmosphere but it must have been considerable. Once cleared for cultivation, cotton itself is a renewable, low impact crop, yet a rough estimate of the CO_2 emissions of the 6.3 million acres dedicated to growing cotton for the British textile industry in 1860 amounts to 257 million tons of CO_2eq (equivalent) per year, a not inconsiderable addition to the emissions of the coal-burning textile factories at home.[1]

British economic command over these land resources in the United States played a significant role in promoting Britain into the hegemonic capitalist economic power in the nineteenth century. It extended the reach of its resource environment by releasing Britain from the confines of its own native

---

[1] This can only be a rough estimate based on the assumption of the emissions of 300lbs of CO_2eq per acre for contemporary cotton production.

land mass. Much has been made of this land both as additional 'ghost acres' by providing a fibre that in part displaced wool and linen, but more significantly, added to the range of clothing available to consumers both at home and across Europe and the rest of the world. It has been calculated seven billion sheep and 700 million hectares of land, or 1.6 times the total surface of Europe would have been required to produce an equivalent amount of textiles in the absence of cotton fibre. If that is an indication of the importance of the release from Britain's national land constraints for economic growth, from a climate change perspective, Britain's distinctive pathway was a combination both of actual woollen textile production mostly from national territorial sheep and cotton with Britain's command over 6.3 million extra-territorial acres. Sheep, combining meat and fibre, have a very different GHG footprint (methane) from cotton, and Britain's unique combination of both in its textile industries constitute its distinctive sociogenic pathway.

The standard historical accounts of the British industrial capitalist revolution, as the globally leading political economy of the 'great divergence', have focused on the key elements of Britain's uniquely characterised coal resources on the one hand, and its colonial and post-colonial economic and political reach in controlling massive new land resources, on the other. It can be no coincidence that explanations of the transformatory emergence of industrial capitalism adopt the key elements of the climate change trilemma: fossil versus renewable energy, competition for land for energy, food and clothing, and generation of greenhouse gases from energy and land use. Historians have asked what was distinctive about British industrial capitalism that placed it at the political and economic forefront of the industrial revolution. It is a many-faceted question that implicitly closes off the search for concepts of generic capitalism, or abstract model capitalism, discussed in the previous chapter. And, in answering the question, historians have pointed to the importance of how Britain's political economy was sited in, and in interaction with, its particular resource environment and extended resource environments over which it gained political and economic command. In so doing, they unintentionally prepared the ground for a sociogenic climate change analysis of British industrial capitalism. There is no chance coincidence between an economic historical account and a climate change account once the interactions between a political economy and its resource environments are placed on centre ground (as in Fig. 1.2). Specific economic transformational developments are at the same time climate changing developments by virtue of those interactions.

To state that the United States is very different from Great Britain is a banality. But if there is one aspect of the contrast in their economic developmental trajectories in the early nineteenth century it can be summed up in one word: land. Once more, the focus here is on one pathway of development in the United States, certainly no comprehensive account of emergent American industrial capitalism. Indeed, the analysis is limited to a Texan twist in the American sociogenesis of climate change, in order to draw out a contrast with the British pathway.

After the Louisiana Purchase, the next great territorial expansion Westwards was the acquisition of Texas, a further 695,662 square kilometres (compared with the surface area of whole of the United Kingdom of 242,495 square kilometres). From a climate change perspective, acquisition of land is central to the analysis. Political and economic control of a resource environment – in this case, Texas – was a critical condition for cattle, cotton, and later oil, to becoming constituent elements of the *American* economy. The process of gaining control over a resource environment, here as an aspect of settler colonisation, was political, military, and by no means solely economic. There were two major obstacles to expansion however: Mexico and Native Americans. The fight for control was complex, stretching over decades until the formal annexation of Texas by the United States as one of the Southern slave states in 1845. In the early nineteenth century, Anglo-American settlers moved in large numbers into what was then Mexico (gaining its independence from Spain in 1821), spearheading territorial expansion. This culminated in direct military conflict with Mexico, and, following the defeat and capture of President General Santa Anna in 1836, the establishment of an independent Republic of Texas. That independence was continuously contested by Mexico, but further settler colonisation, and especially conflicts with Native Americans, resulted ultimately in the annexation of the Republic as a recognised full part of United States territory in 1845. The annexation then provoked the Mexican Wars, which ended not only in Mexican capitulation over the state of Texas thus finalising its boundaries, but also the cession of California, Nevada, Utah, most of New Mexico, Arizona and Colorado, and parts of Oklahoma, Kansas and Wyoming under the Treaty of Guadalupe Hidalgo in 1848. That settled the removal of the Mexican obstacle to political and economic control over the Texan resource environment.

The genocidal destruction and ethnic cleansing of Native Americans from the Texan territory was equally complex, passing through several phases from the years of the pre-Republic, the independent Republic, through even to the post-Civil War period and the Red River War (1874). Moreover, it can only be seen in continuum with the larger historical pattern from the earliest days of colonisation of North America. The Indian Removal Act of 1830 was itself only a major stagepost in the long history of genocides and ethnic cleansing for settler colonisation (Bowes, 2014). This

Act forced the removal of all Indian peoples, notably the Cherokee Nation, to the West of the Mississippi, including into the territory of Texas. Its companion law, the Preemption Act was prototypical for expansionary settler colonisation, by effectively facilitating full property rights to squatter-farmers, legalising de facto illegal occupation. It sanctified forced land dispossession by imposing an alien conception of property rights overriding any Native American traditional rights to their historical living space (Carlson & Roberts, 2006).[2]

The combination of genocidal extermination and ethnic cleansing of Texas is best captured by the brief Presidency of Mirabeau Lamar (1838–41) over the independent Republic. In terms of the control over the plains as an environmental resource, he proclaimed the principle that whites and Indians 'cannot dwell in harmony together. Nature forbids it.' (Cited by Anderson, 2019, p. 180). He moved the capital of the Texan republic into Comanche hunting grounds, naming it Austin; led a Cherokee War in the Red River, and then pursued the Shawnee to consolidate control over the plains. Later, once incorporated into the United States, Native Americans were briefly corralled into unsustainable reservations, and Texas 'finally solved' the Indian obstacles to total territorial control in the Red River War in 1874, following the invasion of settlers into the territory after the Civil War. The remaining Comanche and Kiowa were driven from the panhandle of the plains and upper reaches of the Brazos, Red and Canadian rivers.

From a climate change perspective, aside from Anglo-Americans, a very different invasion accompanied the territorial acquisition of Texas as an environmental resource: the massive expansion of cattle ranching spreading from the

---

2 This law became the permanent bedrock of American land law by further legislation in Congress in 1840.

coastal plains of Mexico and along the Southern United States. Spain, as the colonising country in South and Central America, had long established an agriculture of cattle ranching before introducing it into the Americas (Bishko, 1952; Ficek, 2019). What then became known as Texas longhorn cattle were their direct descendants. Indeed, a law was passed that all wild or unclaimed cattle previously belonging to Mexicans were Texan property (Love, 1916) on their declaration of an independent Republic in 1836. They were the booty won in their territorial expansion in conflict with Mexico. By then, there were already over 100,000 head of cattle in Texas. Expanding territorial control enabled the subsequent development of cattle ranching for the market on an unprecedented scale. Cattle were becoming a major component of the Texan economy, and from 1845, the American Texan economy. There were three main routes for the growth of production in Texas to the major markets for consumption of beef: Westwards to California, Eastwards to the Mississippi River and New Orleans, and Northwards to Kansas City and eventually the Chicago stockyards.

The scale of expansion of methane-producing cattle for climate change is hard to assess. But by the time California had been incorporated into the United States, it has been estimated that around 250,000 beef was transported to San Francisco each year to feed the settlers of the gold rush (Love, 1916). In the same Antebellum period, 50,000—60,000 head of cattle were regularly transported by cattle drive, and then by the same steamships carrying slave cotton, to New Orleans. Direct shipments of cattle from the Texan port of Galveston added to that total (Surdam, 1997). Finally, and more famously, the great cattle drives Northwards, particularly after the securing of the Red River, resulted in a major increase in the trade in cattle. The pioneering and significantly named Shawnee Trail delivered 15,000 head in a single week to Kansas City, and reached an annual total of 57,000 by 1857, protected by a string of forts along the route. By 1866, 260,000 crossed the Red River to deliver beef into Kansas City and further North (Gard, 1953).

With the opening of the railhead at Abilene in 1867, the most famous cattle trail of all, The Chisholm Trail, became the principal conduit of Texan cattle. Even before the Civil War, the 300,000 head of cattle completed the Trail, and by 1870, 600,000 to 700,000 head of cattle were finding their way to the Chicago Stockyards (Gard, 1967). In the two decades of the peak of the Chisholm Trail, 5.7 million Texan longhorns went for slaughter in Chicago (Galenson, 1974). Until way into the 1960s, the genre of the Western was an almost unqualified celebration of cattle-driving, expansionist settler colonialism, with examples such as Howard Hawkes' Red River (1948) suppressing even a glimpse of a Native Americans whose land it had been. This was America's 'manifest destiny' (see Fig. 3.2).

Fig. 3.2. John Wayne in Red River by Howard Hawks.

In surveying the Texan twist to the American sociogenesis of climate change, the political and military expansionism of settler colonialism established a resource environment which in turn resulted in the development of a major contributor to climate change, vast herds of longhorn cattle bred for market on captured land. It was precisely the historically accelerated transition from hunter-gatherer and subsistence agriculture to modern capitalist agribusiness in interaction with a resource environment gained by politics and military power that resulted in a major and distinctive contribution to climate change. But it was more than that. The large scale cattle ranching and distribution to markets, North, South, East and West, contributed to a formation of a meat-eating consumption culture which persists to this day. Representative of ranching economies across North and South America, the United States is the most meat-eating consumption culture in the world today.

Texas and its longhorn cattle spearheaded the early phases of this consumption culture. The advent of the railroad; the subsequent development of refrigeration by the extraction and 'mining' of ice from rivers and lakes; the transformation of the logistics of transport from live cattle to refrigerated 'packaged' meat cuts; these developments concentrated economic power in the Chicago stockyards and large meat packer companies such as Swift and Armour (Cronon, 1991).[3] The Texas longhorns were given 'free range' of the Great Plains after the virtual extinction of millions of bison, brought about especially by the market demand for their hides. Chicago became the 'Great Bovine City of the World', not only supplying beef to the cities

---

3 William Cronon's magnificent environmental historical account of the growth of Chicago as a meat metropolis and its transformation of the Great Plains is interesting *both* for its detailed analysis of the ecological impact on a resource environment *and* for its complete absence of reference to methane and climate change. It was a book of its age, first published in 1991.

of the East Coast of America, but to Great Britain and the world. The extinction of the bison with the Native American subsistence economy related to it and its replacement by the capitalist organisation of the American beef industry in the resource environment of the Great Plains nails the concept of sociogenesis. Bison emit methane just as cattle do. But they were a naturally evolved species, undomesticated or bred. Their methane was 'naturogenic'. They were replaced by a hybrid animal that not only transformed the ecosystems of the Great Plains, but were bred, fed, and transported to market, to be consumed by wage-earning urban consumers across the world. *Their* methane and its upscaling was a peculiarly US capitalist societal phenomenon with its dependency on a distinct resource environment. That is sociogenesis.

The USA reached 'peak beef' in the 1970s, with 90 kilo-grams of beef consumed per capita per year, and a current total world-leading total of 120 kilograms of meat con-sumption per capita per year (FAO, 2013b). It is tempting to assert that President Trump was thinking nostalgically of peak beef when he talked of making America great again, while at the same time personally appearing in advertisements for Trump steaks. So, in terms of the American sociogenesis of climate change, it is not only a question of the historical methane emissions produced by Texan longhorns in the nineteenth century, but the formation of a meat consumption culture that presents the climate emergency challenge of today.

Before leaving Texas, there was yet another twist to its sociogenesis of climate change: oil was discovered in Melrose in 1866, and the first major oilfield opened in Corsicana in 1894. But that is for a later chapter.

Two sociogenic pathways have been traced in this chapter, and the very contrast between driving cattle up the Chisholm Trail across the Red River and coal-powered cotton and woollen textile factory production in England, makes it hard to think that these were contemporaneous, belonging to the same historical world. In their very different ways, they demonstrate how particular societies at particular historical times exploit particular resource environments and in so doing generate greenhouse gases. There is no generic either human or capitalist generation of climate change, only different societal processes in interaction with distinct resource environments. Their atmospheric impact – as measured by natural scientists – aggregates to form the overall human impact of different sociogenic processes. In terms of impact, it may matter little as to whether methane is emitted by five million cattle in Texas or 16 million sheep in England. But it does matter for the climate how it so happened that there were five million cattle in Texas by the 1860s and 16 million sheep in England in 1800.

The British industrial revolution witnessed a new combination between the organic and the inorganic economies, not a suppression of the organic – food, cotton, wool – by the inorganic – coal. Indeed, growth of the inorganic economy drove the expansion of the organic economy with the conversion of new lands to provide its essential raw materials. Britain's relative land scarcity and temperate climate, combined with its ready and 'convenient' resource of coal drove its distinctive trilemma dynamic. Organic energy from wood was replaced by inorganic energy for both domestic and manufacturing processes. But whether for the calories from sugar derived from its own slave and indentured labour colonies or from cotton obtained by its economic hold over US slave plantations, it extended its land environmental resource beyond its national boundaries. From within those boundaries the trajectory sketched above developing from a proto-industrial to an industrial manufacture of woollen textiles had its environmental starting point of an already settled, commercialised and developed agriculture. There was certainly an intensified exploitation of its own agricultural resource environment, but without the land extensification into the 'ghost acres' of the Caribbean and the Deep South of America, the industrial revolution would have been missing some of its most essential ingredients. Britain had a unique and time-specific trilemma dynamic of land, energy, and greenhouse gas generation.

By contrast, the United States was only becoming the United States of today by continuously extending its boundaries, adding vast areas to its political and economic domain, by the Louisiana Purchase, the annexation of Texas, and the Treaty of Guadalupe Hidalgo. Texas has been chosen to exemplify the process of acquiring an ever-expanding resource environment. Land as such, unlike Britain, was no constraint. But gaining political and economic control over that land entailed military adventurism and wars with Mexico and genocidal and ethnic cleansing of Native Americans. From an environmental perspective, in contrast to the industrial revolution, there was an equivalently significant historical transformation from hunter-gather and subsistence agriculture to commercialised agriculture and intensification of the exploitation of land's natural resources. Compared with previous transformations of that kind, it occurred at the speed of light, over a period of decades rather than centuries. The production of beef and the emergence of a meat-eating consumption culture was, at this historical time, the key trilemma dynamic of Texas, feeding the growing urban populations of the United States. Texas above all demonstrates the importance for climate change of the process of acquiring political and economic control over a resource environment in the mere six decades of the nineteenth century before the Civil War.

But Texas, by the 1840s, was also making a significant contribution to the British industrial revolution by exporting high quality cotton from its slave plantations. Hence, when the independent Republic was annexed by the United States, it was controversially recognised as one of the Southern slave states. This link between Texas and Britain illustrates a theme which will be developed later: the attraction of opposites. Land poor Britain acquired economic leverage over land rich United States; temperate climate Britain forged political and economic bonds with the sub-tropical Caribbean and the Deep South of America.

This chapter has explored historical changes of an epoch-changing scale with the consequence of an unprecedented acceleration of the sociogenic emission of greenhouse gases. The key trilemma dynamics, playing out in contrasting ways, of food, energy, materials, and land cast a twenty-first century light on a transformational process of the climate that was both unknown and unknowable at the time. These are histories of the emergence of national inequalities of wealth of an extreme not seen before, which, at the same time are inequalities of societal responsibilities for climate change. But the histories show us just what a massive political and economic development accompanied an equally major change in the earth's atmosphere. It signals that an equally massive scale of economic transformation, as much in consumption as in production, and varying in different political and societal contexts, is required to meet the climate emergency. The unconscious history of past climate change cannot be undone or rewound. But a green social and economic revolution now equipped with a combination of natural scientific knowledge and the historical hindsight of sociogenic analysis has become the order of the day for a new politics for societal economies at national and international scales. A green revolutionary transformation can only be one that addresses those wealth inequalities, both between and within nations, so intimately connected with the sociogenesis of climate change.

4

FEEDING THE CRISIS: HOW OPPOSITES ATTRACT, THE TRAJECTORIES OF CHINA AND BRAZIL

The production, consumption and waste of food contribute nearly a quarter of all greenhouse gases. Between 25% and 30% of all food is wasted. There are an estimated 2 billion people who are either overweight or obese. 821 million are undernourished. So say the environmental scientists of the Intergovernmental Panel on Climate Change, highlighting the significance of food and land for the climate emergency (IPCC, 2019). 'Feeding the crisis' thus exemplifies a particular dimension of the trilemma, with demand for land and water, land use and land use change, being central to the analysis of different resource environments for different societal economies. Nonetheless, an examination of the NDCs (National Determined Contributions) presenting government policies to mitigate climate change at the COP21 2015 meeting in Paris suggests a widespread reluctance for nation states to fully address the climate change risks of food and agriculture.

In the historical context of the previous chapter, Britain's access to New World land for cultivating sugar cane on slave and indentured labour plantations was mentioned in passing. Sugar as a significant source of calories contributed to the development of urbanisation critical for industrial capitalism in Britain (Harvey, 2019; Mintz, 1986). Although conversion of uncultivated land for cultivating sugar, the attendant processes of refining sugar in the 'factories in the fields', and further refining in the metropole, undoubtedly produced greenhouse gases, the main climate change effects were the indirect ones of facilitating urbanisation, notably the centres of manufacturing. In this chapter, the analysis considers the much more direct impact of the production, distribution, markets and consumption of food for generating greenhouse gases. For the USA, by contrast, the historical development of a meat eating culture of consumption based on the appropriation and transformation of land resources initiated a process that continues to have a direct impact on greenhouse gas generation to this day. The contemporary cases of Brazil and China, and the development of food trade between them, are taken as exemplifying contrasting developmental trajectories in interaction with their unique resource environments, with significant differences in both their generation and regulation of greenhouse gas emissions from agriculture.[1] In their very different ways, they represent critical sociogenic dynamics contributing to the present climate emergency. As we shall see, the Amazon rainforest, with its huge significance for the world as a carbon sink, will take centre stage. It is at

---

1 The research for this chapter was funded by an ESRC Professorial Fellowship 'The food-energy-climate change trilemma: developing a neo-Polanyian approach' ES/K010530/1. The research fieldwork included a wide range of interviews with experts, major food producers and traders, NGOs, and government officials, in both Brazil and China.

the centre of the analysis of a perfect climate change mega-storm of politics and economics.

As in the previous chapters, the analysis is driven by the consideration of the interactions between societal economies and the resource environments over which they have some command. In this chapter, particular emphasis will be placed on the two political economies of China and Brazil. Using the term 'political economy' here denotes that economies are treated political entities, and does not merely mean a politics of economies, as if economies were a separate sphere on which governments act. Economies are politically constituted by laws, regulations, taxes and treaties, and are marked by the character of their political formations, their particular political constitutions. It mattered in Brazil whether it was under military dictatorship or democracy, and it mattered in China when the great turn from Maoism to market socialism occurred. These political constitutional changes resulted in fundamental changes in how and where food was produced, traded and consumed. When it comes to feeding the crisis, the political economy of food, the laws on land ownership, the treaties on trade, the ownership and control of water resources, will be seen to be central features of the socio-genesis of climate change.

At the same time, a key dimension to this analysis concerns the finitudes of a given society's environmental resources. In the case of food, availability of agricultural quality land, ground and surface water, and sun are the key finitudes of concern. As will be seen, however, environmental resources available to an economy, although naturally 'given', may also be politically defined. So, for example, land use change in the Amazon biome may be legally restricted from deforestation, or in China the area of agricultural land may be protected from being taken for industrial, commercial, housing or other non-agricultural uses.

The analysis of societal interactions with finite resource environments concentrates on some key dimensions:

- the changing patterns of land holdings, their ownership and control;

- different agronomies related to land-holding such as scale and mono-cropping;

- policies of food security and self-sufficiency;

- food export-orientation;

- last, but by no means least, cultural differences and transformations of societal norms of consumption.

The politics of food are at play across all of these dimensions, and, to that extent, the analysis is of 'politically instituted' economies of food.

The climate change consequences of these instituted economies of food, situated in their different ecologies, are also diverse across some key dimensions. Land-use change, where and how it happens, is of immense significance. Different agronomies related to land-use and land use change, how and where what meat (beef, pork, poultry) are produced, intensive use of nitrogen phosphate fertilisers including for rice, all have contrasting levels of GHG generation, from CO_2, as well as nitrous oxide (N_2O), and methane (CH_4). Whether a society's culture is predominantly beef-, poultry-, pork-eating – or indeed vegetarian – has major climate change consequences.

Finitudes of environmental resources, instituted economies of food production and consumption, and agronomic GHG generation together constitute the sociogenesis of climate change. Different societal dynamics generate distinctive climate change impacts. The fact that different societies exhibit different dynamics has critical policy implications for the innovation of different, societally relevant, regulatory responses for climate change mitigation, which we reflect on in the conclusion.

The chapter is constructed as follows. In schematised form, the developmental trajectories of China and Brazil are examined separately systematically comparing the key dimensions of societal interactions and their economies of food production and consumption. The consequential GHG signatures for each country are contrasted, showing how different societies generate different mixes of climate changing gases. The results of these comparisons are then summarised in tabular form.

These national trajectories then critically intersect from the early twenty-first century, with Brazilian exports to China developing a novel and significant reconfiguration of their respective political economies of food. In terms of their contrasting resource environments, especially of fertile land, water and sun, opposites attract. This leads us to question the appropriate unit of analysis for understanding the societal dynamics of climate change, arguing that neither producer country nor consumer country, but the new producer-consumer configuration is the appropriate spatial scale. In doing so, an addition to the analytical framing is developed to take account of these societal changes involved in the sociogenesis of climate change: configurations of Production, Distribution, Exchange and Consumption (PDEC for short) (Harvey, 2007). The attraction of opposites results in a new PDEC configuration between Brazil and China, which is graphically represented to summarise the analysis. The chapter concludes by drawing out some of the policy implications, both intra- and inter-national, for climate change mitigation.

THE CHINESE SOCIOGENIC TRAJECTORY

With a population of 1.35 billion, in spite of a relatively large land mass, China has one of the lowest per capita amounts of agricultural land in the world, at 0.08 hectares (World Bank, 2014a). Deserts, high altitude plateaus, and mountainous areas mean that cultivatable land is concentrated along the Pacific shores and in the South and especially South East of the country. Moreover, much of its land is naturally poor in organic content, a 10th that of the United Kingdom, making its potential yield significantly lower than that attainable in more nutrient rich soils (Interview, Fusuo Zhang, May 2014). Its water resources available for agricultural production are even scarcer, at a quarter the world average, a fifth of that of the USA, and one-fifteenth of Brazil (World Bank, 2014b). Again, its water resources are very unevenly distributed, with the North East being water poor compared with the South and South East (Lu et al., 2015).

If these are the 'naturally given' finitudes for Chinese agriculture, they were thoroughly modified by the agricultural regimes instituted by pre- and post-revolutionary China. Here, we focus on the key dimensions of landownership and food and agriculture policy, particularly self-sufficiency and food security. Since 1949, successive changes in landownership were uniquely and distinctively politically driven (Ye, 2015). These transformations describe a remarkable spiral, each radical reform echoing a previous phase of land-holding even in its novelty: individualisation (1949) – three-stage collectivisation (1953–1978) – re-individualisation (1978–1989) – re-collectivisation (1997–). Following the Revolution, 300 million peasants were given full private property rights to the land they tilled, resulting in extreme fragmentation of land, but addressing the pre-revolutionary concentration of landownership by landlords and rich peasants. Enduring rural poverty and lack of development then led to three stages of progressive collectivisation, from mutual aid teams and low level cooperatives (1953–1956), to cooperative-collectivisation (1956–1998), finally to People's Communes (1958–1978). In the short cooperative-collectivisation period, private landownership was replaced by full property rights of the collective, further expanded in scale with public ownership of land under the People's Communes. During these later phases, major transformations in agricultural infrastructure were developed in irrigation, roads, mechanisation, and seed provision. Following the turmoil of the Cultural Revolution, the major post-Mao Tse Tung reform re-instated individualised household farms under the Household Responsibility System, with the major difference that the local state retained ownership of the land. Households became leaseholders under leases initially of 15 years, then gradually extending, reaching a maximum of 70 years for certain types of farming. This has again resulted in extreme fragmentation, with typical landholdings of less than one third of a hectare. These changes in landownership have critical consequences for climate change, shaping the society's interactions with the environment in the production of food.

Egalitarian land distribution combined with incentives and subsidies directed at increasing production for the market, typifies the hybrid economic forms of market socialism. But, once more, the scale limitations of 230 million farms have triggered a process of re-collectivisation from the late 1990s, notably with Farmer Professional Co-operatives. In sharp contrast to the earlier collectivisation phase, this has been achieved by opening up of markets for land leases, where the peasant household rents out their leases to third parties, while the state continues to own the freehold. In Polanyian terms, this exemplifies a 'politically instituted market', where what can be traded and by whom, is prescribed by the central state (Zhang & Donaldson, 2008). These new forms of co-operative, moreover, have been complemented by a form of agricultural capitalist enterprise, the Dragon Head Enterprise, again a politically constructed entity, mostly involved in upstream agricultural activities of processing and distribution, but also in intensive livestock rearing (Schneider, 2016). The recent phases in landownership transformation have always been combined with a uniquely Chinese mode of socially engineering the rural-urban migration under the *hukou* registration system, with the urban population exceeding the rural in the second decade of this century. A significant number of peasants, now urbanised, complement their insecure and volatile urban incomes with rents from their traded land-leases (Ye, interview, 2016). Yet, however 'planned', a major consequence of these land reforms and migration controls has been an ageing and feminising of the 'left-behind' rural population (Ye, Wang, Wu, He, & Liu, 2013). This presents a major challenge to the dominant current policy of modernisation, scaling-up and professionalisation of agriculture.

These major transformations of the organisation of landownership were significantly driven by a dominant food policy of food security which, until joining the World Trade Organisation in 2001, was equated with food self-sufficiency. The drive to feed the growing Chinese population was a paramount political imperative, particularly following the traumatic famines of the past. Alongside the reforms of the Household Responsibility System, therefore, policies were introduced to increase yields. Environmentally, the most significant of these were the industrial strategy to develop China's own nitrogen phosphate industry, on the one hand, and to subsidise farmers to purchase and use chemical fertilisers, on the other. While remarkably successful in raising Chinese agricultural productivity until recently (van der Ploeg & Ye, 2016), these policies have led to an environmental catastrophe. Overuse of fertilisers has undermined the prospect of both increasing yields and absolute agricultural production of key crops (Norse & Ju, 2015; Zhang et al., 2014). As Fusuo Zhang put it: 'A farmer just buys a bag of fertiliser and dumps it on the land, making sure that there's enough by dumping too much' (Interview, May 2014; Liu et al., 2013). The quantity of fertiliser per hectare in China is now many times that of Europe and the USA (Liu et al., 2013). China exceeds the combined use of chemical fertilisers in the USA and Northern Europe, and accounts for more than 30% of total world use (Zhang et al., 2014). The FAO now estimates that up to 30% of agricultural land has been degraded, and water resources widely contaminated (FAO, 2013a; Strokal et al., 2016).

When characterising China's sociogenic climate change from agriculture, it is important to recognise the significance of rice as an emitter of two powerful greenhouse gases, methane and nitrous oxide now amplified by over-fertilisation. This is a linked production-consumption specificity, a policy of food security and self-sufficiency especially applied to rice as a major cultural component of national diet. The environmental impacts are multi-dimensional: acidification of the soil, eutrophication of surface water, and an augmented level of nitrous oxide emissions, now accounting for 10–15% of China's GHG footprint. The subsidy to 250 million smallholders, without the necessary skills and technologies, led to uncontrolled use of fertilisers. Landownership combined with food policy created a distinctively Chinese sociogenic climate change phenomenon.

China responded significantly to this domestic agri-ecological crisis, again with a societally distinctive set of policy measures (Mu et al., 2014; Liu et al., 2015). Policies have been developed targeting the three key dimensions of land, water and fertiliser use (Wang et al., 2010). In complete contrast to land-rich Brazil, legislation was directed against the constant reduction of its limited agricultural land from conversion to industry or urbanisation, with a 'red line' against it falling below 120 million hectares (Wang, Chen, Shao, Zhang, & Cao, 2012). So legislation is aimed at limiting the conversion of agricultural land into urban, infrastructural or industrial uses. It also aimed to conserve the quality of agricultural land against further degradation. The ecological crisis of China's water resources has in turn been addressed by three 'red lines', relating to competing water uses (agricultural, industrial and domestic), the efficiency of water use, and protection against fertiliser and other pollution (Zuo, Jin, Ma, & Cui, 2014). Given China's high level of reliance on energy-intensive abstraction of groundwater for agriculture, water efficiency also promises a potential reduction in energy demand as a measure of GHG mitigation. Finally, from 2015, measures have been adopted with the ultimate objective of capping the total amount of fertiliser use, with zero increase from 2020, preceded by a limitation of 1% increase per annum from 2016 (Liu et al., 2015). This policy has been combined with widespread experimentation in agronomies to increase yield with reductions in emissions from nitrogen fertilisers. Some of these experiments have involved intensive support to Farmer Professional Cooperatives, raising levels of knowledge and use of new hybrids and rotational systems (Zhang et al., 2013, 2014).

A striking feature of these environmental regulations is their focus both on Chinese finitudes of land and water, and on the peculiarly Chinese sociogenic characteristics of pollution and GHG emissions from agriculture. However, experts interviewed all stressed the significant barriers to implementation of these policies, of which the fragmentation of farms and rural out-migration, and changing demographics of the left-behind rural populations were particularly daunting. Moreover, modernised and scaled-up intensive pig-rearing enterprises, relatively unregulated, were now adding a new source of pollution and GHG emissions (Strokal et al., 2016).

Pigs form a useful bridging link to the other major shift in Chinese food and agriculture policy, raising quite different aspects to sociogenic climate change. From the late 1990s, it had become clear that China would no longer be capable of feeding itself. In part that was because China engaged in a nutrition transition involving a much wider section of the population eating more meat (Gale, Hansen, & Jewison, 2015). *Food security no longer equated with food self-sufficiency.* The political imperative expanded beyond meeting the "basic needs" of food security (Garnett & Wilkes, 2014; Hansen & Gale, 2014; Huang & Rozelle, 2009). As with rice, China's traditional consumption culture of eating pork as a pre-eminent meat is a critical dimension of its sociogenic climate change. But westernisation of many consumption patterns has also challenged that tradition and is now driving a rapid growth in eating beef (Bai, Wahl, Lohmar, & Huang, 2010). Thus, from 1980 to 2015, per capita increase of annual pork consumption has grown from 12 kg to over 40 kg, poultry from less than one to over 10 kilograms, and beef, from under one to five kilograms (Hansen & Gale, 2014). The GHG impact of eating pork is less than a 10th that of eating beef, and poultry even less (Gill, Feliciano, Macdiarmid, & Smith, 2015). Different countries have different nutrition transitions, with consequently different planetary impacts. Above all, in China per capita consumption then has to be multiplied by 1.35 billion to appreciate the scale of the impact of its distinctive nutrition transition.

In 2001, China joined the World Trade Organisation, partly in order to meet the changing and rapidly expanding food demand. Since then, China has progressively widened the scope of its imported food. Again key policy decisions shaped this transition, with imported whole soyabeans as the major

source of animal feed for pork production. The state promoted a strategically important national meat industry, with
targets for rapid intensification and modernisation (Sharma,
2014; Brown-Lima, Cooney, & Cleary, 2010). Already a
major exporter of soya to Europe and elsewhere, within
10 years China had doubled Brazil's exports, now accounting
for over half of its trade (FAOSTAT, 2015). Critically,
China's agri-industrial strategy was to process whole soyabeans for animal feed by its national industry, rather than
importing soymeal. It produces the overwhelming proportion
of its pork domestically (Schneider, 2011; Schneider &
Sharma, 2014; Sharma, 2014). The consequential impact on
Brazilian land-use and land-extensification, to be discussed
below, has been significant, with 11 million hectares now
dedicated to producing soya to feed China's pork production
and consumption. Many now argue that Chinese demand has
been a primary driver of increased deforestation and carbon
emissions from agriculture in Brazil (Fearnside & Figueiredo,
2015; Peine, 2013; Nepstad, Stickler, & Almeida, 2006).

The production-distribution-consumption configuration
for beef has taken a quite different trajectory from pork. The
increasing proportion of beef in overall meat consumption has
been delivered to a significant extent by the expansion of
multinational fast-food retailers, McDonalds, Burger King,
and KFC (Expert interviews, May 2016; Ma, Huang, Fuller,
& Rozelle, 2006). One expert recalled how she was always
rewarded with a McDonald's beefburger when she achieved
the highest marks in her class at school. National herds have
been declining from the 1990s, only partially compensated by
increased yields from a low productivity base. The typical size
of herd in China is under five head of cattle, because of the
continued domination of small and fragmented land holdings.
The domestic cattle industry has been slow to change
(Waldron, Jimin, Huijie, Xiaoxia, & Mingli, 2015).

So, unlike pork, China has imported beef on an increasing scale. Once more, as with soyabeans, Brazil has responded. Major global Brazilian multinationals have stepped in to fill the demand gap, especially following the opening up of direct imports to the Chinese mainland, rather than indirect ones either through Hong Kong, or the major smuggling trade via Vietnam and Laos of 400,000 tonnes annually (Waldron, Brown, & Longworth, 2010). Since 2010, Brazilian imports have exploded (Fig. 4.1). There has also been a marked shift from importing whole frozen carcasses for butchering and processing within China, to pre-prepared packaged cuts ready

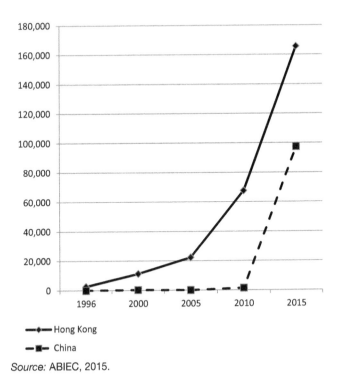

Source: ABIEC, 2015.

Fig. 4.1. Brazilian Beef Exports to China in Tonnes.

for retailing (Interviews with Brazilian MNCs, December 2015 June 2016). There is a remarkable parallel here with the nineteenth-century development of the Chicago beef supply chain discussed in the previous chapter. Today, increasing Chinese beef consumption has led to minimally increased demand for land in China. Cattle for China are reared on an increasing scale in Brazil and Australia, and an increasing proportion of added value is captured by both Brazilian meat exporters and MNC retailers operating in China.

Growing and changing food consumption in China, in particular its distinctive meat transition, clearly has major implications for GHG gas generation, alongside the ecological crisis of over-fertilisation and intensification. It is important to signal, however, that the shift from the dominance of basic staples has not only been towards more meat, but also towards more fruit and vegetable varieties, the consumption of which has quadrupled from 100 kg per capita in the mid-1980s to over 400 kg in 2011, double that of European consumption (Gill et al., 2015). Moreover, China has recently issued guidelines to limit the growth of meat consumption, suggesting that the politics of consumption retains a strongly national character. Yet, overall the departure from food self-sufficiency, with only wheat and rice, no longer even maize, retaining the political objective of 95% domestic production, has been remarkable and rapid (Expert interviews, May 2016). However, as we have shown, China is distinctive in both production and consumption, and also distinctive in its trading patterns. China has now politically forged a dominant bilateral trading relationship with Brazil. Its food sociogenic driver of climate change is thus both within its own national territories and with its international trade relations. As with the British command over environmental resources in the USA and the Caribbean for cotton and sugar in the eighteenth and nineteenth centuries, China now has its 'ghost acres' in Brazil for soyabeans and beef, commanding access to many vast areas of land, and expanding outwards the commodity frontiers cultivated land. It does not do business anyhow, anywhere in a global market, but in a directed and channelled way, with a country which itself is distinctive for its export oriented agriculture, to which we now turn.

THE BRAZILIAN SOCIOGENIC TRAJECTORY

Although later to become strategically connected to China, the Brazilian sociogenic trajectory from land-use, land-use change and agricultural production of food could scarcely be in stronger contrast to China in terms of societal interactions with its environmental resources. As already noted, Brazil has many times more cultivated land and potentially cultivatable land, water and solar energy per capita than China. Much of the potentially cultivatable land – as a Brazilian 'gift of nature' – only became an effective agricultural resource as a consequence of high-tech agronomic and biotechnology innovation. From early in the twentieth century agricultural expansion has been driven by state-sponsored research including globally prestigious agricultural universities (Harvey & McMeekin, 2005; Hopewell, 2016). Brazil could now be described as 'the Middle East for food', ranking first in the world as exporter of beef, poultry, coffee and orange juice; second going to first for soya; third for corn; and fourth for pork (Hopewell, 2014; Wilkinson, 2009). Its carbon footprint signature corresponds to its geopolitical status: already by 2009, 65% of its GHG emissions derived from agriculture and deforestation, compared with China's 15–20%, USA, Russia and Europe at 10% or less (UNDP, 2012). It is sociogenically in a league of its own for inducing climate change from agriculture.

In order to understand the dynamics of this distinctive sociogenesis, the same key dimensions will be considered as for China: scale of agricultural operations, linked to land use and land use change; state policy in relation to food production and trade; changing consumption patterns, domestically and internationally; and the emergent state and self-regulatory dynamics to mitigate climate change. It is important to stress that there is a Brazilian domestic dynamic, including its own meat consumption transition, which combines with distinctive Brazilian economic organisation of its export trade, whether for soya, or varieties of meat.

Initially, it is worth reflecting on the contrast between China and Brazil. While China was losing agricultural land to urbanisation and industry – one estimate was for 14.5 million hectares between 1979 and 2005 (Lichtenberg & Ding, 2008) – and then to pollution (see above), Brazil was expanding its agricultural land by 5 million hectares *every year* in the 1990s (Fearnside, Figueiredo, & Bonjour, 2013), through deforestation of the Legal Amazon. Since 2000, the rate of extensification (changing virgin into cultivated land) through deforestation has reduced remarkably, but to a level still amounting to some 800,000 hectares per year (Hecht, 2012). The two principal climate change sociogenic drivers related to land use in Brazil have been extensification and scale of production, of which the former has received overwhelming attention, particularly with respect to the Amazon biome (Hecht, 1993; Fearnside, 2001, 2005, 2008; Fearnside & Figueiredo, 2015; Fearnside et al., 2013; Nepstad, Stickler, & Almeida, 2006).

The processes and phases of extensification have been complex. But in very broad terms, from the 1970s to the mid-1990s extensification involved timber extraction followed by very low density pasturage of poor quality (one head of cattle per hectare). This created a vast reservoir of what has now been deemed degraded pasture land (estimated between 50 and 100 million hectares). Since the welcome reduction in the rate of extensification (discussed below), two processes have followed, the expansion of soy production and intensification of cattle stocking, also releasing more land for alternative cultivation (soya, corn, sugarcane). Given the distinctively Brazilian focus on extensification, exploitation of the degraded pasture reservoir (indeed its restoration including reforestation), have been routinely portrayed as offering a sustainable way forward for growth in agricultural production (Cardoso et al., 2016; Latawiec, Strassburg, Valentim, Ramos, & Alves-Pinto, 2014; Macedo et al., 2012; Martha, Alves, & Contini, 2012a; Pereira, Martha, Santana, & Alves, 2012). Bold claims are made that with more efficient use of existing and historic pastureland, *all* demands on future agricultural production could be met until at least 2040 without further conversion of natural habitats (Strassburg et al., 2014). In this peculiarly Brazilian perspective, the sins of the past created the space for the virtues of the present. More sceptical voices point to a continuing pressure, especially from supplying soyabeans to China, for the further displacement of cattle ranching into the virgin Mato Grosso cerrado and Amazon biome by the expansion of soya cultivation into existing pastureland (Fearnside et al., 2013). And, as we shall see, a change in political regime in Brazil has unleashed a whole new wave of deforestation and land extensification.

From the 1930s, if in very different ways in different periods, the state has played a key role in the process of extensification, by no means always directed at the expansion of agriculture or agricultural exports. Under the Generals (1964–1985), the creation of the reservoir of low-grade or degraded pasture from the 1970s was driven by a state objective of gaining strategic territorial control during the Cold War to meet threats of peasant-led revolutions in Latin

America (Oliveira, 2016). Thus, provisional landownership was given to clearing land in the Amazon and cerrado, on condition that minimal cultivation followed deforestation, a condition met by creating grassland and having one head of cattle per hectare. 'Pasture was a state strategy not to produce protein but to occupy land.' (Interview, JBS, Dec 2015). Apart from addressing issues of landlessness and rural displacement in the South and Centre South, a succession of policies across political regimes stimulated the conditions for the subsequent dramatic development of Brazilian agriculture for global markets in soya and beef. Vargas' 'March towards the West' was followed by an alliance between Japan and Brazil for the expansion of soy production in the cerrado, in particular in Mato Grosso, now for the global market (The Program for the Development of the Cerrados, 1975–1982). During this period, soy cultivation received heavy state subsidies. Up to 2001 and the entrance of China, exports of soymeal were predominantly for Europe, and soy oil to Asia. State-promoted soy-extensification was further supported by the policies of 'Brazil in Action' 1996–1999, and 'Forward Brazil', 2000–2003. As Fearnside has stressed, the state development of infrastructures of waterways, roads, rails and ports has throughout this long period created a 'dragging effect', pulling in more land for cultivation through extensification (Fearn-side, 2001). Finally, with the entrance of China into the WTO, state-to-state negotiations established favourable trading terms, including currency swaps for trading in soy to escape dollar hegemony (Hopwell, 2016b; Oliveira, 2016; Wilkinson & Wesz, 2013). These trade terms underpinned the massive expansion of land producing soybeans for the Chinese pork industry, so playing a key role in Brazil's current GHG emissions from agriculture.

Aside from the physical infrastructures and export and trading state objectives, the Brazilian state has a long tradition of development of its agriculture knowledge infrastructures, placing it at the knowledge frontiers as much as, and oriented towards, its land frontiers. The Luiz de Queiroz College of Agriculture (ESALQ), a premier agricultural college and part of the University of Sao Paulo, was established in Piracicaba in the heart of one of the sugarcane growing areas, providing research and training from as early as 1901. In 1971, the Brazilian Agricultural Research Corporation (EMBRAPA), a public corporation funded by government, was established. It created a decentralised network of research and technology centres, dedicated to developing different crops adapted to the frontier regions of extensification (Correa & Schmidt, 2014; Martha, Contini, & Alves, 2012b). The Sao Paulo Research Foundation (FAPESP), a state funded research organisation, financed the development of genomics and biotechnology associated with Brazil's primary crops, leading the world in the genomics of plant pathogens notably of Brazil's global citrus industry (Harvey & McMeekin, 2005).

Although a very different political system from China, therefore, these different dimensions of state intervention underpinning the extensification process (state security, land-ownership, physical and knowledge infrastructures) placed Brazil in a position of the leading world food-producing power it has now become. Moreover, extensification, and a further shift to export orientation from the 1970s was accompanied by a major change in the scale of agricultural operations. This too reflected the distinctive model of Brazil-ian development combining state with domestic agri-capital and the multi-national commodity traders: an economy standing on three legs. Brazil's industrialised high-tech agri-culture manifests the typical 'tripod' (tripé) characteristics of other sectors of its economy (Evans, 1979). The Brazilian agricultural sector is also strongly split between the large-scale export-oriented producers and the small and medium scale farms, more directed towards the domestic market. This alliance between large domestic capital, multinationals and the state significantly shaped the subsequent environmental policies and regulation of land-use in Brazil. Again, this is not a capitalism-in-general basis for generating climate change, but a distinctive political economy in a unique resource environment.

In the most recent 2006 census of landholdings, the 1% of farms with holdings of over 1,000 hectares occupy 45% of all cultivated area, while the 49.4% of farms with holdings of less than 10 hectares occupy a mere 2.2% of cultivated area. Farms of over 100 hectares, mostly those involved in export oriented supply chains, constituting 10% of all farms, occupy 80% of all Brazilian farmland (USDA, 2016). Although there is substantial variation in soy farm size, the process of expansion into degraded pasture for export-led soy production in the Centre West (Mato Grasso) involved the emergence of large, even mega-scale, farms (Macedo et al., 2012; Mier y Terán Giménez Cacho, 2016), such as the Roncador Group farm with 150,000 hectares, and the Amaggi Group Tanguro farm with 80,000 hectares. The scaling up of units of production, moreover, was closely associated with the formation of supply chains dominated by the ABCD group and indigenous Brazilian agri-capital (Garrett, Lambin, & Naylor, 2013; Jepson, Brannstrom, & Filippi, 2010). To appreciate the significance of these scales, these mega-farms are up to *450,000 times* larger than the average Chinese farm, and even the typical Brazilian small household farm is more than 100 times larger than its Chinese counterpart.

A parallel development has occurred with beef production, typified again at one end of the scale by Gruppo Roncador that added cattle to its soy production in an integrated agronomy, with a mega-herd of 50,000. By Brazilian standards, in the key beef producing area of Mato Grasso, the small scale cattle farms range from a few hundred head to 2,000, whereas in terms of quantity of animals and land, the dominant ranches raised herds of up to 15,000 (Cerri et al., 2016). Again, these herds are on a magnitude of scale greater than anything to be found in China. However, the dynamics of scale are complex, and, as with China, politically and economically shaped. Thus, to prevent the earlier pattern of extensification at the fringes by small farmers being displaced by large ranchers, a policy of Settlement Projects has secured a substantial and continuing presence of smallholders (Pacheco & Poccard-Chapuis, 2012; Soler, Verburg, & Alves, 2014). However, these small farmers in turn are dominated by the beef processors, notably Marfrig and JBS, now also owner of Bertin. There is a distinctive economic organisation of small farmers providing large ranches with calves for fattening, which then go direct to the processors via the pinch-point of their abattoirs. The insertion of smallholders into global and national-scale supply chains, under asymmetries of power in the market exchange, has been described as a new form of exploitation by transnational corporations (Pereira, Simmons, & Walker, 2016).

The processes of farming extensification, degraded pasturage, cattle intensification, and then expansion of both soy and cattle production have therefore led to a distinctive character of agriculturally driven sociogenic climate change in Brazil. Cattle intensification, releasing degraded pasture through 'land saving' has been widely heralded as mitigating climate change from extensification (Cohn et al., 2014; de Oliveira Silva et al., 2016; Martha et al., 2012a; Strassburg et al., 2014). At the same time, however, the overall beef herd in Brazil has increased five times to its current level of over 200 million head from the early 1970s (Pereira et al., 2012). JBS slaughters over 1000 head of cattle per day, and Marfrig a similar number. Recent studies have demonstrated that

GHG from cattle is consequently overwhelmingly the most significant for climate change, rather than land clearing and deforestation. Cattle produce 75%–90% of agricultural greenhouse gases emissions (methane and nitrous oxide) from enteric fermentation and excreta (Cardoso et al., 2016; Cerri et al., 2016). But a word of warning. Soy production on previously degraded pasture, although nitrogen fixing and hence potentially beneficial in terms of Brazilian production, is dedicated to animal feed, whether in Europe or China. Soy production is directly connected to new configurations of meat production and meat consumption with consequential climate change implications, but does not appear on Brazil's climate change balance sheet. It is the new configuration that matters for climate change, not the soy grown in Brazil versus the meat produced in Europe or China.

Although much attention has focused on export-driven agricultural growth, especially from China, as a primary source of deforestation and climate change (Fearnside & Figueiredo, 2015; Fearnside et al., 2013; Peine, 2013; Oliveira & Schneider, 2016), it is important to recognise Brazil's own domestic consumption dynamic and its meat transition. Although beef exports have risen dramatically by 672% from 1995 to 2013 from a very low base, domestic consumption has also grown by 41% over the same period, and still comprises 80% of total beef production (Fig. 4.2). Where exports grew by 1.6 million tonnes per annum over this period, domestic consumption grew by 2.3 million tonnes per annum.

From a sociogenic perspective, moreover, as discussed below, domestic supply is less tightly regulated than global export supply chains, and more likely to be responsible for the continuing levels of deforestation and low density pasturage. Again in contrast to China, Brazil's meat consumption culture is dominated by beef symbolised by the national institution of the *churrascaria* (meat barbecue) (Ribeiro & Corcao, 2013;

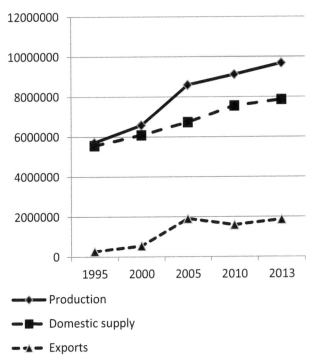

Source: FAOSTAT (2016).

Fig. 4.2. Brazil's Bovine Meat Production, Domestic Supply and Exports (tonnes, per annum).

Carvalho de Rezende & Alberto Rodrigues Silva, 2013). So, comparing meat transitions, Gill and colleagues have shown that per capita Brazilians eat double the amount of beef in 2011 that they did in 1961, at around 40 kg per year by 2013 (ABIEC, 2016). Now also annually consuming a similar quantity of poultry per capita, their total per capita meat consumption exceeds European levels, and is on an upward curve in the direction of USA levels of meat consumption. By 2011, Brazilians were consuming 92.6 kg per capita, compared with Chinese consuming 52.4 kg per capita. Given the significance of beef consumption with its far greater GHG impact, Brazilian per capita CO_2 emissions from eating meat is almost 10 times greater than China, although, of course, with a much smaller population of some 250 million (Gill et al., 2015).

The scale of emissions from Brazilian livestock is simply staggering. According to a recent calculation (Pereira, de Santana Ribeiro, da Silva Freitas, & de Barros Pereira, 2020), livestock were responsible for just over *1 billion* (1,185,645,379) tonnes of CO_2 equivalent in 2015, with the rest of agriculture adding a further 272 million tonnes of CO_2 equivalent. This is *20 times* more than the mere 66 million tonnes CO_2 equivalent for all Brazilian power generation, or the 75 million tonnes of CO_2 equivalent for all metal and chemical industries. When it comes to the climate emergency, it is its GHG hoofprint that singles Brazil out and presents the biggest challenge. If Chicago became the bovine capital city of the world in the nineteenth century, Brazil has become the bovine superpower of the 21st.

If Brazilian food production and consumption is socio-genically distinctive for climate change, so too and relatedly were its mitigation policies, both in their focus and in their organisation. Note the past tense. The fall of Dilma Roussef, and the election first of President Temer (2016), and even more so, President Bolsonaro (2018) made these policies past history, as will be discussed below. When they were being developed, whether for soy or for beef, the predominant almost exclusive focus had been on preventing deforestation and extensification, particularly into the symbolic Amazon biome, and much less so into the Mato Grosso cerrado. As for politico-economic organisation, so too for climate change mitigation, the policies manifested a distinctive blend of state and multi-national corporations in their organisation. The overarching state policy, originating in the 1960s as the Forest

Code, had been strengthened successively, most critically with
the establishment in 2012 of the Rural Environmental Regis-
try (CAR), backed up by the Ministério Público Federal and a
dedicated policing force (IBAMA). Cadastral registration of
legally held land, and defined areas of reserved and indigenous
land was enforced in particular by real time satellite monitoring of land-use change (INPE and PRODES). These Brazilian state instruments had been combined with post-Kyoto
international instruments directed particularly at deforestation, the REDD+ and REDD++ carbon-offset trading policies
(Reducing Emissions from Deforestation and Forest Degradation) achieving some notable successes typified in Acre State in
the Amazon biome (Agrawal, Nepstad, & Chatre, 2011;
Alencar et al., 2012; Hall, 2008; Nepstad et al., 2014). These
policies and technologies of monitoring and regulating land use
change in real time, using National Institute of Space Research
(INPE) satellite tracking, were unique in the world, represent-
ing pioneering environmental supervision.

These state and international governmental measures were
significantly complemented and coordinated with a distinctively Brazilian combination of state and domestic and international multi-national corporations engaged in preventing
the sourcing of food from the Amazon biome and from newly
converted virgin land. Thus, for soya, the Roundtable for
Responsible Soy was established (2006), followed by the more
effective Soy Moratorium (2006). The latter, interestingly,
was established in part as a consequence of an intervention by
Greenpeace, indirectly through McDonalds in Europe, in turn
exerting pressure on Cargill, so subsequently embracing major
soy producers, traders and processors (Abiove, Amaggi,
Aprosoya, Cargill and Unilever) (Interviews with all the above
named, August, September, December 2015). The moratorium had recently been extended to 2020, and from an early
stage had had government involvement, in particular the CAR

and INPE land-use change monitoring. Likewise for cattle, a combination of state and multinational corporations, this time exclusively Brazilian, established a similar sustainability roundtable, the Grupo de Trabalho da Pecuária Sustentável (2009) and developed the so-called G4 agreement (2009), initiated in Pará state, but then extended to the adjacent states. These state-self-regulatory combines for beef were also designed to prevent the sourcing of cattle from the Amazon biome and newly converted virgin land (Interviews with JBS and ABIPEC, December 2015 January 2016).

A key feature of this politico-economic organisation of climate change mitigation concerned enforcement and implementation, on the one hand, and land coverage on the other. Notably, the multinationals worked with environmental NGOs (The Nature Conservancy, Greenpeace, WWF, Instituto Centro de Vida), certainly to enhance their sustainability branding for domestic and international markets, as well as state enforcement of CAR.[2] Cargill, JBS and Marfrig all use INPE satellite tracking and their own dedicated software (versions of DEGRAD, DETER and PRODES) to police their supply chains in real time. Across all the large scale soy and cattle producers, and their respective trade bodies, there was a widespread insistence that self-regulation on its own was insufficient without the complementary coordination with CAR and the enforcement agency of the Ministry for Federal Prosecution and IBAMA. Cargill refused to use aggregated supply from upstream small producers in its supply chain that it cannot trace. Marfrig and JBS excluded any transgressors of CAR from their supply chains – JBS barred over 2000 ranches in 2015 (Gibbs et al., 2016). However, these big players

---

2 JBS announced that its pioneering Novo Campo project secured branding for sustainable hamburgers from Arcos Dourados, McDonald's brand operator in Latin America (17 August 2016).

engaged in these state-cum-self-regulatory combines only control 50–60% of the market, destined for export. Domestic supply falling outside either state or corporation capacity for real time monitoring and enforcement no doubt contributed to the continuing levels of deforestation.

> *Even if you put JBS and Marfrig together in the Amazon region they only purchase 40% of the total cattle. So you have 60% of the market operating without rules.*
>
> (Interview, JBS, 1 December 2015)

Finally, a few demonstrator projects were oriented to sustainable intensification of agriculture, such as JBS's Novo Campo and the BRF-Sadia Lucas do Rio Verde farm reducing the carbon footprint of both beef and soy in integrated agronomies. These promising ecological innovations are marginal to the main regulatory orientation towards limiting extensification, on the one hand, and are of limited countervailing influence to the overall growth in meat production and consumption, domestically and internationally, on the other.

The Bolsonaro-Trump Climate Change Accelerator Pedal

Politics matter. All through this analysis of the Chinese and Brazilian trajectories, the role of the state, political constitutions, the laws and regulations have demonstrated just how political are economies of food, and consequently how central politics are to the sociogenic analysis of climate change. The elections of President Trump (2016) in the USA and President Bolsonaro (2018) in Brazil, each in their own way, have demonstrated just how significant a change in political direction can be in intensifying the climate emergency. They have not only reduced the possibility of achieving a global reduction in GHG emissions, but have put the whole political dynamic dangerously in reverse.

In the wider picture, President Trump's withdrawal from the Paris Agreement on climate change, his promotion of coal and oil exploitation, and his systematic dismantling of the Environmental Protection Agency and regulatory control have been the most dangerous for the future of the planet. President Bolsonaro had imitated his puppet-master by cutting the budgets of the National Policy on Climate Change by 95%, of IBAMA as the police force controlling deforestation of the Amazon, and of the agency tackling forest fires. He has dismissed the evidence from INPE tracking the increase of deforestation, and actively promoted the commercialisation of the Amazon. As a consequence, in 2018–2019, 4,200 square kilometres of forest were felled in Brazil, an increase of 50% from the previous year (Escobar, 2019), and the latest figures from July 2019 to August 2020 show an even more alarming acceleration to 110,088 square kilometres in just the one year.

But it is the particular Trump-Bolsonaro combo that concerns us here, the perfect climate change mega-storm. In pursuing his 'America First' trade war with China, Trump provoked China to impose a 25% tariff on US soyabeans in 2019. The climate change consequence has been immediate, massive and directly linked to Bolsanaro's devastation policies for the Amazon and for the Mato Grosso cerrado. In 2016–2017, the United States had exported 59 million tonnes of soyabeans to China compared with 61 million tonnes from Brazil. In the following year, after China had imposed its tariffs, US exports of soya to China reduced by 90%, and with Brazil expanding its soyabean production, its exports to China almost doubled (Gale, Valdes, & Ash, 2019). The Trump politics of trade combined with the Bolsonaro politics of environmental destruction to expand demand for Brazilian soya. That is what is pushing the devastating figures of deforestation cited above. It is the perfect climate change mega-storm, concentrating the China-Brazil link to such an extent that China now completely dominates Brazilian soya production, and Brazil has a near monopoly of China's consumption. It is an accelerating spiral of climate change.

CONTRASTING SOCIOGENIC TRAJECTORIES AND THE ATTRACTION OF OPPOSITES

This chapter has focused on food rather than energy or other economic activities, but the analytical framing is relevant to all areas of economic activity. The trajectories analysed above have highlighted some key dimensions especially, but not exclusively, relevant to agriculture and food production: political systems; economic configurations of markets, producers, processors and traders; land holding property rights and scales; and consumption patterns. In a Polanyian spirit, the distinctiveness of both socio-political movements generating climate change and the counter-movements mitigating climate change was emphasised. These complex dynamics are an integral part of understanding sociogenic climate change. The contrasting trajectories of China and Brazil across these dimensions are summarised in Table 4.1.

One key conclusion from this analysis is that different trajectories of interaction between socio-politico-economic systems and their resource environments generate different GHG footprints. This is at the core of the concept of sociogenesis. Each dimension of this interaction (political systems, landholding, agronomies, consumption etc.) is important in its own right. But only in combination, at the societal level, do they together, and over historical transformations, generate their distinctive dynamics of climate change. How and which

Table 4.1. Trajectories of Sociogenic Climate Change: China and Brazil.

	China	Brazil
Resource environment	Relative agricultural land scarcity, reducing through urbanisation and industrial development. Uneven water distribution, with areas of high aridity.	Relative land abundance and unconverted forest and savannah. Relative abundance of water, but under threat from climate change.
Political economic system	Central command economy with market socialist reforms from late 1980s.	Military dictatorship, development state and 'tripod' political economy of state, large domestic and international corporations.
Land ownership and scale	Highly fragmented minuscule household farms from 1989, with increasing fluidity in land leasing, underpinned by continued state land ownership.	Bifurcated landownership between small/medium household farms with mega-farms dominating landownership.
Food security and self-sufficiency	Policy of food self-sufficiency until joining WTO in 2001. Key grain crops (rice, wheat) self-sufficient. Increasing imports especially of soya, corn and meat.	Food self-sufficient and secure, although high levels of inequality.

Table 4.1. (*Continued*)

	China	Brazil
Agricultural productive systems	Intensive agriculture with high chemical inputs, and low mechanisation. Stalled infrastructure development. Small-scale production.	Expansion through extensification, followed by exploitation of degraded pasturelands. High-tech mechanised industrial agriculture on large scale farms.
Domestic and international market orientation	Domestic for food, globalised for manufacturing, IT, clothing, etc.	Strong export orientation. Dominant global food exporter for meat, soy, orange, coffee....
Consumption and meat transitions	Increasing consumption of meat from a low average level, dominated by pork, but beef emerging.	Meat eating culture, especially beef, on an upward per capita curve already above average European levels.
Greenhouse gas footprint signatures	Nitrous oxide from overfertilisation, methane from rice, pig slurry.	CO_2 from land use change and deforestation. Methane from cattle enteric fermentation.
Climate change mitigation	Central command 'Red Lines' on agricultural land reduction, chemical fertiliser use, water pollution and use. Directives to curb meat consumption.	State regulation on land-use change and deforestation, combined with state-corporate self-regulation restricting further land exensification especially in Amazon biome.

greenhouse gases are emitted relate to the organisation of land holdings, and consequently to agronomies at different scales. Rice or wheat production in China, even with small-holdings, can be regionally monocropping, but with totally different agronomies from the large-scale monocropping of soya or beef in Brazil. Politics runs throughout, across all dimensions. And all are conditioned by the naturally given resource environments. Analysed holistically in a Polanyian manner, moreover, the contrasting movements of unsustainable economic growth in Brazil and China have been modified to some extent by nationally distinctive counter-movements of environmental regulation. Sociogenic analysis embraces both movement and counter-movement. Finally, in both cases it remains a wide open question whether their respective policy responses – including their COP21 Paris commitments – adequately recognise the scale of the challenge of growing and changing food demand, and the consequent pressures on land use and land use change.

In addressing the sociogenic character of climate change and the distinctiveness of national trajectories, it might be argued that the significance of globalisation – whether of economic activity or of the planetary aggregation of greenhouse gases – is being underplayed. The Brazil-China linkage has been highlighted for a purpose, because on the one hand China's food policy and needs may indeed create a demand for imported soya, and, on the other hand, Brazil was already in a path-dependent trajectory of exporting soya to Europe before its rapid growth of exports to China. Brazilian export trade of food is certainly international, but it is not uniformly global. Indeed, whether for beef, poultry, soyabeans and soyameal, its trade patterns contrast strongly both with Argentina and other Latin American countries, but also with the USA (Koopman & Laney, 2012). The specificity of Brazilian and Chinese trajectories, it can be argued, also generates the specific and distinctive trade connections between them. Opposites attract. That was the pre-existing context for the Trump-Bolsonaro combo effect. What had originally been an attraction of opposites then became a forced marriage.

Whether for domestic or international markets, the theoretical perspective developed here advocates a configurational approach, integrating production, distribution, exchange and consumption, for soya or beef, domestically or internationally. Interestingly, the emergent configurational connections between Brazil and China differ as between beef and soy (see Fig. 4.3). They differ as a consequence directly of Chinese policy, environmental resources, and capacities, and of the role of Brazilian and multinational agents. Thus, China only imports soybeans from Brazil, processes them, and grows and up-scales its own pork industry. In contrast, Brazilian beef multinationals combine the roles of processor and trader, including provision of packaged and processed products ready for the supermarket shelf in China. The economic organisation of the trade connections for soy and beef, which also has its GHG generation consequences as to where and how GHG is generated, thus exemplifies the need for a sociogenically refined rather than amorphously 'global' approach. Politics deeply condition and shape the flows of trade, the links between producer and consumer countries, and hence the processes generating greenhouse gases.

CONCLUSION: UNITS OF ANALYSIS AND POLICY IMPLICATIONS

A key feature of the COP21 Paris Agreement (2016) was the Nationally Determined Contribution to ensuring that the world control their emissions in order to prevent global warming by more than 2 degrees. Thus, the negotiating

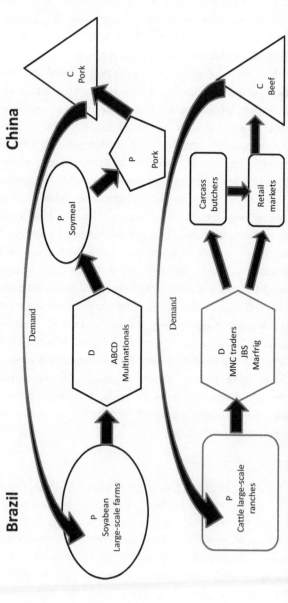

Fig. 4.3. Opposites Attract: The Production (P)-Distribution (D)-Exchange-Consumption (C) configurations for Beef and Soya.

framework recognised the continuing significance of states in their capacity to control emissions on their national territory. Conversely, when a major state reneges on its commitments to use this capacity, there are severe consequences for the world in the absence of other means of enforcement. Indeed, the significance of a nation state policy perspective is borne out by the above analysis of China's Red Lines and Brazil's Forest Code and moratoria.

However, the sociogenic perspective on climate change highlights two important, and often connected, deficits in this perspective: a one-sidedly productivist account of emissions and emitters (leaving out consumption and demand); and the failure to address sustainability regulation of international trade (Norse, Lu, & Huang, 2014). Ironically, the sustainability self-regulation discussed above for McDonald's 'sustainable hamburgers' and the McDonald-Cargill-Soy Moratorium initiative, for all its many limitations, partially addresses this double deficit. Multinational global traders respond to markets, NGOs, and environmental movements in consumer countries when they seek sustainability branding of their products. In many interviews, across a range of such companies, it was stressed that they could not sell half a chicken without sustainability credentials in one market and the other half with sustainability credentials in another market, as it were. Unlike the chicken (soy, beef, or whatever), sustainability credentials and reputation are seen as indivisible, at least to many large-scale, multi-country, producers and traders. But, when the political climate changes, as it has in the USA and Brazil, even these limited mitigating market pressures are undermined. There is now evidence that Europe – particularly after its failure to include environmental regulation in its trade agreement with the Mercosur – is now importing both beef and soy from illegal and newly deforested zones in Brazil (Pereira, de Santana Ribeiro, da Silva Freitas, & de Barros Pereira, 2020).

This chapter takes configurations of production, distribution, exchange and consumption, at whatever scale, local, national or international, as its unit of analysis. It does so, arguing that the dynamics driving climate change are best understood in configurational terms. In so doing, a false antithesis between producers or producer countries and consumers or consumer countries is avoided. So it matters that China is consuming more and more meat; and it matters how and where, by what agronomies, animal feed and meat is produced in Brazil. They are sociogenically significant, separately *and* together. Policies need to be focused on the dynamics of configurational change, whether these are entirely within national boundaries, or whether they involve the specific connections of international trade. Climate change mitigation policies need to be adapted to configurations and configurational transformations. They entail a sustainability politics of consumption as much as of production and trade. In taking this approach, bilateral trade agreements related to the dynamics connecting producer with consumer countries, such as those between China and Brazil, can focus on what needs to be done on both sides of the connection. Given the scale and rapidity of changing food demand and agricultural production and their significance for climate change, radical new policy approaches adapted to their sociogenic specificities are ever more urgent.

5

FUELLING THE CRISIS:
ELECTRIFYING SOCIETIES,
MOTORING IN SOCIETAL SPACES

The British industrial revolution and settler colonialism of the United States, each in their own way, rapidly accelerated changes in the earth's climate at a pace never before witnessed in previous human societies. In Chapter 3, a hint was dropped pointing to further waves of acceleration: the first significant exploitation of oil fields in Texas in 1894. In this chapter, two major accelerants of climate change are considered: the electrification of domestic homes and industry, and the use of oil for terrestrial transport. The ubiquity of the technologies of power generation using coal or gas, or of the combustion or jet engine for consuming oil, might seem a challenge to the concept of sociogenesis of climate change. After all, from a natural science standpoint of anthropogenic climate change it matters not a hoot whether a car burns petrol in the USA or India or a plane flies from London or Paris to Moscow or Washington, any more than it matters whether a cow farts in Brazil or Australia. The impacts on the earth's atmosphere are the same or similar.

Yet, as was argued in Chapter 3, when it comes to how coal is burnt, it did matter decisively where the right kind of coal was located geographically, how and for what purpose it was burnt, and why, historically and socially. The British industrial revolution and domestic heating were primarily responsible for the acceleration of climate change caused by burning coal. Likewise, in the United States the acceleration in climate change arose from the historically unprecedented transformation of land use from hunter-gatherer and subsistence societies to full-blown commercial agriculture of cotton and cattle. In both cases, climate change acceleration was the outcome of the particular interactions between political economies and their resource environments.

The same conceptual analysis is equally applicable to electrification and mass transportation. As with the previous analysis, politics and political systems are of central significance. But there is an added aspect when turning to the politics and political systems behind the societal generation of greenhouse gases from electrification and mass transportation. In both areas, governments have historically made strategic decisions, including ones governed by military or defence objectives, in promoting the infrastructures critical for power generation and transport. These strategic decisions are conditioned by the context of national resource environments, the presence or absence of coal or oil reserves, or of suitably dammable rivers. Consumer choices or preferences were not directly responsible for bringing about these decisive and large scale transformations generating climate change.

Likewise, strategic and governmental decisions are also required to meet the scale and pace of change required to overcome the climate emergency. The consequences for consumer choices may be habit-disturbing and radical, but we as citizens require our governments to make the profound and system-wide changes necessary to avoid the

climate catastrophes that are already knocking on our
doors. Sociogenic analysis can tell us how different societies
have got us to where we are in order to identify the scale and
nature of the societal actions required to get us out of the
climate emergency in which we are currently situated. At the
same time, however, this sociogenic analysis demonstrates
how societies, by their previous strategic directions, have
created obstacles and resistances to the necessary change.
Not the least of these are the inequalities in the use of
electric power or oil-propelled transport both within and
between nations, which will be the particular focus of the
next chapter. Rich nations and the rich within nations are
responsible for the hugely greater part of global emissions.
Societal inequalities and inequalities between nations present a major obstacle to the radical change necessary to save
the planet.

ELECTRIFYING SOCIETIES

*Communism is Soviet power plus the electrification
of the whole country, since industry cannot be
developed without electrification.*

VI Lenin (1920)

Lenin's pronouncement is as good a starting point as
anywhere for exploring how distinctive societal trajectories of
climate change are generated by 'electrification of the whole
country'. Different political economies in interaction with
their distinctive resource environments pursue electrification
with very different strategies. Infrastructures of power generation and transmission entail massive, long-term and coordinated investments which to a great degree lock countries into
their historic modes of electrification. In all societies, capitalist

or communist, developed or developing, the state has always played that strategic role in electrifying society. There is certainly no uniform 'capitalocene' pattern of electrification.

Under the Tsarist government, and as a notably under-developed economy, small steps had been taken to build electricity power stations near Moscow and Petrograd. For fuel, these were dependent on the dominant imperial power, as Russia imported coal from the Welsh coal fields. Lenin shared Siberian exile with a notable electrical engineer, Gleb Krzhizhanovsky, and already by 1914 had imagined a tech-nological utopian future. He envisaged 'the transformation of dirty, repulsive workshops into clean, bright laboratories worthy of human beings' and the liberation of millions of 'domestic slaves' by the introduction of household light and heating (Cited by Coopersmith, 2016, p. 153). The First World War had severed the access to Welsh coal, resulting in a fuel hunger stretching into the first years of revolutionary Soviet Russia. At the same time, in the early years of the civil war, White Russian forces had also cut off supplies of coal from the Donets region and oil from the Baku oil fields. To survive the fuel hunger, the Moscow and Petrograd power stations were adapted to burn local wood and peat. Peat extraction became a huge and labour-intensive undertaking to keep the electricity flowing.

But that could never have been a long term prospect to fulfil Lenin's vision. An alternative vision of a central com-mand economy reliant on native energy resources became the political imperative of the revolutionary government. The goal was energy autarky. In 1920, the State Commission for the Electrification of Russia (GOELRO) developed the very first instance of the new planned economy with a supremely ambitious programme for the electrification of the economy. It aimed to quadruple the pre-war electricity generation with a combination of 10 major hydroelectric power stations, with 30 regional power plants, mostly in the industrialising European Russia centred around Petrograd and Moscow. In the event, given the overreaching ambition for building massive dams, only three hydroelectric plants were built by 1930. Even after Lenin's death, electrification of the society remained a dominant ambition for subsequent five-year plans. However, there were continuing political struggles both within the Communist Party and outside, over the structuring of the infrastructure. Early in Lenin's vision, electrification had aimed to overcome the 'metabolic rift' between town and country. The early emphasis on a centralised regional, industry-oriented, system of power generation, was countered by pressures to decentralise and build a network of smaller power stations feeding more rural areas leading to a modification of the state planning. This political and technological conflict was also expressed in terms of energy source, whether hydroelectric power should be based on large dams over major rivers (so-called 'white coal'), or whether there should be mini-hydroelectric generators on a more decentralised basis (so-called 'green coal').

In the event, by 1930, only three large dams were built, the most notable being the Volkhov hydropower station, supplying Leningrad (Petrograd). With the development of the New Economic Programme, there was a degree of decentralisation, including 13 mini-hydropower stations in the Moscow region. The more centralising vision of multiple large scale hydropower stations came up against industrial capacity, as well as technological and political limits. Overall, the early infrastructural foundations of these first decades of Soviet planning set the direction of development whose imprint lasts to this day (see Fig. 5.1). Geography of environmental resources combined with the politics of centralised planning. Coal from the Donets region and oil from the liberated Baku oil fields came to dominate the energy sources of Soviet

electrification from this earliest phase, with hydroelectricity
taking a distinctly third place. A survey of energy sources for
the 78 power stations surveyed in 1925–1926 documented
that 70% of fuel was either coal or oil (Coopersmith, 2016).
This was an effect of the national resource environment within
which the distinctive Soviet politics and technologies of electrification played out.

During the same period as the electrification of the Soviet
Union, leading economies of the world, the USA, the UK,
Germany and others, were witnessing a major new phase of
electrification bringing it towards its full climate-changing
impact. Innovations in the introduction of turbines replacing
rotary engines and the development of high voltage transmission cables transformed the scope and scale of electrification. Regional grid systems embracing hundreds of miles were
developed in those countries with extensive territories
(Hughes, 1983). The United Kingdom became the first country to have an integrated national electricity grid serving the
whole country. In order to achieve this unifying scale of
operations, the grid was brought into state ownership under
the Central Electricity Board. It was Britain's first nationalisation and undertaken by a Conservative government, as
Herbert Morrison (the architect of Labour's subsequent
nationalisations) wryly observed.

Apart from this huge expansion in scale, two further
climate-changing aspects of regional electrification emerged.
Firstly, the new grids integrated central city areas with the ever
burgeoning suburbs, increasing massively the market for the
new industries of domestic electric equipment – vacuum
cleaners, kettles, heaters, cooking ovens, washing machines,
refrigerators, radios and so on. This ever-expanding range of
equipment created new societal differences in energy requirements to support them. The toaster, for example, complemented the emergence of mass produced steam-baked white

sliced loaves, proliferating in the USA or UK, but virtually absent in France with its distinctive bread culture, as was, until recently, the electric kettle. *Cultures of production enmeshed with cultures of consumption.* In societies where space is at a relative premium – Japan, the Netherlands or the United Kingdom – there is an adaptive virtue of designing small and neat. This contrasts with societies where there is a socially promoted perception of spatial abundance such as the US, where lack of spatial social constraints privileges designing large whether for refrigerators or cars. The average size of an American refrigerator is double that of Europe or Japan, with consequently greater energy demand. Of course, rich people command more space than poorer people, and equip themselves accordingly – but that is for the next chapter to discuss in greater depth. Here, we focus on societal differences layering on top of inequalities of wealth within or between different nations. National climate differences can, at least in part, account for the widespread domestic presence of air-conditioning, highly energy intensive, whether in apartment blocks of New York or the shanty-town dwellings of slums in Delhi. Over 90% of households in the US or Japan own air-conditioning units, compared with 10% in Europe, or 60% in China. Cooling of work-place buildings in the USA accounts for over half the total air-conditioning energy requirements for the whole world (IEA, 2018, Fig. 1.7). The number of residential air-conditioning units has nearly quadrupled between 1990 and 2016. Keeping more and more cool with more and more global warming.

A further significant source of societal variation is the gendering of labour markets. The emergence of markets for domestic electrical equipment coincided, in some societies but not others, with the disappearance of domestic servants and married women increasingly participating in the labour market including in the very industries producing the new equipment (Glucksmann, 1990). These are societal differences which then have climate change consequences through the replacement of electric energy for human labour. So, domestic electrification of societies expanded the energy requirements dramatically beyond the basic provision of lighting, but did so in societally varied ways. These societal differences serve to emphasise just how deeply embedded electric energy requirements are in the very fabric of the social life of nations.

Second, and depending directly on the regional resource environments, the emergence of large-scale regional or national grids integrated numerous sources of energy to ensure the stability and flexibility of the supply load to meet both domestic and industrial demands at different times of the day and year. One of the key requirements for the new technologies of turbines and high-voltage transmission lines was high energy intensity, whether from dams or fossil fuels. Proximity to sources of either kind of energy was a key determinant of the energy mix or monopoly. Generally, hydroelectric power required large well-fed dams with high rate of fall. But whether in the USA or Germany, even major new hydroelectric constructions were combined with coal-fired power stations to sustain the regional grid requirements. In Germany different combinations evolved. The Bavarian Alps provided the necessary height and drop to create a dam at Walchensee to drive multiple turbines, but required an interconnected coal fired power station to ensure flexibility and continuity of power supply. By contrast, after the First World War, Germany had been deprived of access to some of its hard coal mines and was obliged under war reparations to export some of its hard coal reserves. To ensure national energy security, Rheinisch-Westfälisches Elektrizitätswerk (RWE), the major electricity supplier, part-government owned part-private, expanded its electricity supply for the Ruhr regional grid by building a massive power plant at the Goldenbergwerk. It was strategically placed on top of the brown-coal open cast lignite mine, lignite being the most climate-changing form of coal. In both cases, geography of environmental energy resources, whether water or coal, was decisive.

Likewise, in the USA the massive Conowingo hydroelectric dam was interconnected with coal fired power stations placed close to coal reserves, under the Philadelphia Electric Power Company, expanding into a regional grid network in the 1920s. Yet more famously, the Tennessee Valley Authority was established by Theodore Roosevelt as a strategic economic intervention, part of the New Deal, to raise the United States out of the Great Depression, as well as to supply electricity to rural areas, domestic homes, and industry. At the outset, confronting vigorous opposition from private electricity providers, Roosevelt established in law the principle that if rivers were a public good, then so too should hydropower be. In the context of the current pandemic, with much talk of New Deals and state intervention in the economy, this project of constructing a series of dams on the Tennessee River was seen as an economic and social objective, not at all as an environmental benefit to the planet's atmosphere. That would be an anachronism. It certainly demonstrated the power of state intervention in how to confront an economic emergency, on a scale dwarfing the contemporary state ambitions to mitigate climate change. And yet, as a paradigm example of the interaction between a political economy and its resource environment, this triumph turned into an ironic twist of fate for the sociogenesis of climate change. By the 1950s, the TVA had built the largest coal fired power station in the world, and had become the largest coal consumer in the world (McCraw, 1976). As with the Philadelphia Electricity Company, it combined its huge hydropower capacity with coal-powered generation that

outstripped the hydro in capacity by over five times the
kilowatts by 1975, benefitting from the proximity of Appalachian coal. Moreover, this expanded capacity was driven
first by the wartime needs to provide power for the adjacent
aluminium industry building airplanes, and second, by the
development of the secret Oak Ridge nuclear installation that
was part of the Manhattan Project. Post-war, having provided electricity for uranium processing, this trajectory led to
the TVA constructing a nuclear power plant at Sequoyah, so
completing a hydro-coal-nuclear combination.

Finally, the resource environment for Britain's development
of the national grid relied almost exclusively on coal, in the
absence of a river geography capable of supporting high-
volume, high fall-rate hydropower. For the electrification of
society in this interwar period, the supply of coal for power
generation tripled from 5 to 15 million tonnes by 1938. By
then, electricity generation was the third most important
consumer of coal, following domestic consumption and the
iron and steel industry. By 1980, consumption for electricity
generation had risen to 86 million tonnes, and with the decline
in domestic consumption and the increased electrification of
industry, reached the astonishing proportion of 72% of all
national coal consumption (Minchinton, 1990). This exemplified a sociogenesis of climate change from an electrification
of society in which there was an almost total reliance on the
national environmental resource of coal.

These four societal examples of electrification, both in
consumption of electricity and in its production demonstrate a
huge societal level of commitment to a major climate-change
inducing transformation. The different political economies
exploiting different resource environments developed quite
distinctive modes of electrification. The very creation of grids
interconnecting industry, the military and domestic households meshed society together in historically unparalleled

ways. In the case of the USA, grids linked the construction of war planes with toasting bread or vacuuming carpets. New industries of domestic electrical equipment emerged, employing millions, often women. They produced what were heralded as 'labour-saving' devices, that is, replacing low-carbon human energy with high carbon electrical energy. Electrical equipment became embedded in all the routine social practices of daily life: cleaning, cooking, home entertaining, and food preservation. It is not an exaggeration to say that electricity held societies together in radically new ways. This phenomenon has been characterised as a social and political 'lock-in' (Unruh, 2000). Whether at the level of government, of major corporations, or of domestic households, people have become locked-in to ways of life with multiple interconnecting ramifications. The very term 'lock-in' was created to highlight the huge challenge to the de-carbonisation of society, held together by all these levels of mutually reinforcing ties.

And lock-in is an important concept. But it should not be overstated. Wars, external shocks, and internal political conflict can all induce modifications, if not radical transformations, of these heavily embedded societal electricity systems. In the case of Brazil, as we have already noted, the oil price shocks of the early 1970s stimulated the switch out of imported petrol and into biofuels, saving the Brazilian economy $69 billion over the course of the two early decades of the policy. Some societies remained, to greater or lesser extents, locked-in to the critical infrastructures and patterns of consumption of the interwar years. Others, some quite dramatically, did 'unlock' only to establish new infrastructures of electricity provision with their own inbuilt tendencies to lock-in. In terms of consumption, the ever-expanding range of domestic electrical equipment points to a continuing, ever-deepening societal lock-in.

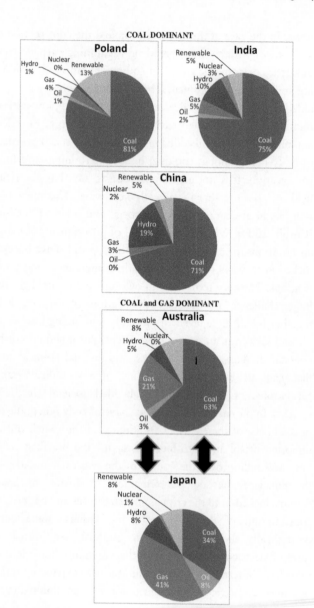

Source: EIA, 2019.

Fig. 5.1. Societal Variation in Energy Sources for Electrification.

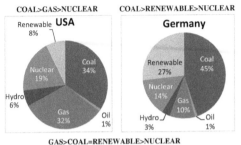

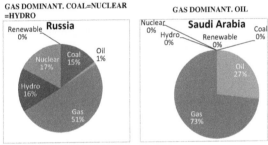

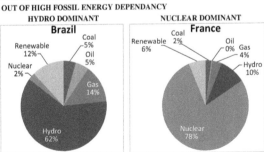

Fig. 5.1. (Continued)

To appreciate the full range of variation between societies in their exploitation of resource environments, Fig. 5.1 groups different societies according to their dominant energy sources. In doing so it is worth emphasising the climate change significance of the different sources of energy. It is also worth emphasising that neither domestic nor industrial consumers of electricity have any direct choice over what energy is used to generate their electricity: the choice is political and societal. Hard and brown coal (lignite) have nearly double the CO_2 emissions of natural gas by unit of heat generated, with oil midway between. The coal dominant countries (China, India, Poland and Australia) thus have a distinctively higher greenhouse gas signature from their generation of electricity. In marked contrast, Saudi Arabia, directly benefitting from their distinctive resource environments, is overwhelmingly reliant on gas and oil. And of course, all fossil energy is climate changing, as against renewable or nuclear power generation.

The USA, Germany and the United Kingdom are all still heavily reliant on fossil energy, coal, gas and oil, to a large extent (67%, 55% and 53% respectively). However, both the United Kingdom and Germany provide examples of a shift out of their historic extreme dependency on coal. The very dominance of coal in the case of the United Kingdom and the power of the National Union of Mineworkers provoked a right-wing Conservative government under Margaret Thatcher to attempt to crush union power, close down deep-mined coal, and switch to national resources of North Sea and imported gas in the so-called 'dash for gas'. As Mitchell (2011) has argued strongly, the power of mining unions, derived in part from their solidarity as a workforce enduring the most hazardous conditions, was a force for democracy in a way that oil, as a natural resource, has been a force for autocracy. The extent of dependency on coal in the United Kingdom gave the working class a distinctive political leverage, which Thatcher was determined to crush. The current characteristic of energy consumed for electricity generation thus reflects the outcome of that political struggle, out of a historic 'lock-in'. In the United Kingdom and especially Germany with its Energiewende (energy turn), renewable energy has become an increasingly significant example of a partial escape from fossil energy lock-in. Germany now has the largest percentage of renewable energy in Europe (at 27%, notably domestic solar), followed by the United Kingdom (23%, notably wind turbines). But, in the case of Germany, another shock, this time external, has provoked a shift out nuclear energy following the Fukushima nuclear plant catastrophe in Japan. At the same time, and against environmentalist opposition, Germany is reverting to style by opening new major coal fired power stations, such as Dateln 4. Likewise, and with increasing controversy, it is enhancing its dependency on gas imported from Russia, with the planned Nord Stream 2 pipeline. To that extent, Germany's carbon lock-in continues.

The two stand-out examples of escape from fossil carbon lock-in are Brazil and France, Brazil by virtue of exploitation of its huge environmental resource from hydroelectricity. France has only a 6% reliance on any kind of fossil energy. Its nuclear energy accounts for 78% of its electricity generation, supported by a further 10% from hydropower, and renewable energy just so far contributing a fraction more than its minimal use of fossil energy. Yet, this distinctive pattern was to a significant extent the effect of the external shock of the Middle East oil crisis of the 1970s, its lack of national coal resources, as well as its national military and security ambitions to become a nuclear power. It made its decisive switch out of carbon lock-in and into nuclear energy as a response to oil shocks and Cold War politics. Accidently, it was a sociogenic pathway to low-carbon electricity, a marked example of climate change mitigation. If France's post-war economic development had instead relied on fossil energy for electricity, industrially and domestically, the planetary impact would have been significantly higher.

Japan, as the third largest economy in the world by GDP, is unique amongst the big global players for its lack of an energy rich national resource environment, with only 10% of its energy being 'home grown'. For its electricity, at its peak, nuclear power as a national resource generated 29% of its electrical power. But, at this point, the ambition had been to increase nuclear power to at least 50% by 2030, to meet its national climate commitments. Before 2011, the Japanese Ministry of Economy, Trade and Industry planned to reduce coal generation of electricity by more than half. Then an earthquake struck, and the Fukushima nuclear disaster shook Japan. Before the disaster, coal accounted for a quarter of Japan's electricity generation. It has now risen to a third, and Japan is the third largest importer of coal in the world, together with its imports of natural gas. So, in this case an external shock has induced a sharply increased fossil carbon lock-in, even if Japan's coal-fired power stations are amongst the most efficient in the world. Moreover, just as Brazilian soy was for China, so Australian coal is for Japan. Brazil land rich, China land poor; Australia fossil energy rich, Japan fossil energy poor. If Brazil is the dominant food exporter in the world, so Australia is the world's largest coal exporter. Just as opposites attract in the case of the 'marriage' between Brazil and China, so Japan accounts for nearly half of Australia's total coal exports, and Australia exports 70% of its total coal production. As a supreme climate change irony, Japan now consumes as much Australian coal as Australia consumes itself. Hence the arrows in Fig. 5.1 finger these 'partners in climate change', binding Australia and Japan together socio-genically ever more tightly. Moreover, just as increasing demand for soy is pushing the food frontier ever outwards into the Amazon and cerrado, so increasing coal demand is pushing the coal frontier also into indigenous peoples' land in Queensland, threatening its environment and the planet.

The Australia-Japan partnership in climate change highlights another feature so important in understanding both the sociogenesis of climate change and a source of resistance to its mitigation. Baldly, Australia has fossil energy assets and Japan does not. If catastrophic climate change is to be avoided, Australia's assets will in large part have to be buried, and Japan will have to release itself from carbon lock-in. The technical term for this is 'stranded assets', a major source of national wealth would be rendered valueless in market terms, but invaluable for the planet. The term, however, demands a much broader concept which embraces the Brazil-China partnership as well as the Australia-Japan one. Environmental resources, whether of fossil energy or of fertile land, are unequally distributed across national societal spaces. There are not only huge wealth inequalities between nations but also huge natural resource inequalities, whether of fossil fuels, fertile land, water, sun, wind, minerals, or whatever. The brief survey of societal electrification in different countries in this chapter, in particular the variation between countries in their sources of the energy, is a direct reflection of these environmental resource inequalities. In the absence of coal or oil reserves, Japan and France took radically different directions, not least because Japan is sitting on a tectonic plate fault line jeopardising the safety of nuclear power. Societal electrification was shaped by national riches or poverty in territorial coal, oil and gas, or water gradient resources, with all the relative mixes in between. As one extreme example of an extreme political regime, in the 1930s Nazi Germany attempted to achieve complete energy and materials autarky by developing liquid fuel and gas, as well as synthetic rubber and fabrics, by hydrogenising its nationally rich coal resources

(Tooze, 2007). In terms of the overall analysis of the socio-genesis of climate change, the interaction between particular political economies and their unequal and varied resource environments, or their ability or inability to access resources through trade or conquest, is critical for understanding the climate emergency and resistances to change. We revisit this inequality dimension in the next chapter, but now turn to oil and transportation through societal space.

MOTORING IN SOCIETAL SPACES

Fig. 5.2. Cars Made America.

In 2014, Bob Dylan produced a video advertisement for Chrysler cars. Dear Reader, if you want to hold on to a culture hero, DO NOT click on this link: https://www.youtube.com/watch?v=qOotVKvKrdk. 'Cars made America', he crowed (Fig. 5.2). 'You won't find a match for the American road' he boasted, adding as an afterthought 'and the creatures that live on it'. He beat President Trump in claiming what made America great: not beer, he observed (Germany); not the watch (Switzerland); not your mobile phone (Asia); but the car. And he is, well, sort of right. In The USA, there are almost 800 cars per 1,000 people, compared with 519 in the United Kingdom, or the high 500s for France, Germany or Japan, and a mere 188 for China (although China now has the largest car fleet in the world, with 360 million vehicles). But, in its significance for climate change, perhaps the more important statistic is the amount of road fuel consumption per capita. Bob Dylan didn't include in his lyrics the fact that Americans are by far the biggest gas guzzlers in the world. They consume *four to five times* more road fuel per capita than people in European countries. Typical of an oil rich country, now supplemented by shale oil and fracking, the price of road fuel is less than half that of France, Germany or the United Kingdom, partly as a consequence of fuel tax regimes. And they walk, cycle and use public transport less, all by a large margin. As an example of the motorisation of society, America is way out in front on the sociogenic road to climate change.

This American profile is much more than an effect of inequalities of wealth, of America being the richest country in the world. As with electrification, there are societal cultures of production and consumption with huge differences in the way societies are organised across a range of dimensions: national spatial scale, patterns of urbanisation, organisation of alternative systems of transport (rail, bus, cycleways, flight), road use laws, and taxation regimes. Also similar to electrification, the infrastructure of roads provides the condition of possibility of mass car consumption and use. In the case of roads, despite prehistories of private tolls, infrastructures are pre-eminently publicly owned, and, with minor exceptions (for example, France) largely free access. Consumers can choose – often within nationally distinct markets – the cars they privately own. But, as with electricity generation, they do not choose through market purchases the kinds of roads they drive on. The paradigmatic example of market capitalism – the family car – only exists in conjunction with public infrastructures strategically established by the state. The sociogenesis of climate change arising from the motorisation of society is a joint state-market enterprise, a characteristically societal phenomenon.

The pre-eminent national case of such road infrastructure systems is the 'matchless' Interstate Highway network in the United States. Although partly developed for defence objectives, this network exemplifies the long-duration multi-modality of capitalism, and the interdependence between public infrastructural innovation and market product innovation (Flink, 1970; Lewis, 1997; McNichol, 2006). The Federal-Aid Highway Act, 1956, financed the construction of 41,000 miles of new roadway through the Highway Trust Fund, which was based on hypothecated petrol, diesel, and tyre taxation, after many alternatives had failed. President Eisenhower, a Republican, eventually drove through this major expansion and transformation of the road network. It both interconnected cities, and, through feeder roads, critically and expressly addressed the isolation of rural communities previously cut off from the rest of American society for months of the year. The peculiar state financing has been described as

> ...a virtual Möbius strip of money: the more cars travelled, the more gas they consumed; the more gas meant more money to build more miles of highways; which allowed more cars to travel more miles and consume more gas.

(Lewis, 1997, p. 127)

As an engineering feature, it rivals the Great Wall of China as the most visible human construction to be seen from space, and 'the largest engineering project in history'. Significantly, state road innovation drove market innovation for the design of cars as much as vice versa, an example of complex interaction between political and market processes (Flink, 1988). Suspension, aerodynamics and engine capacities radically adapted to their new road infrastructural environments, in contrast to early models, like the model T Ford with its high suspension suited to rutted dirt roads. Ironically, the architect in the Senate of the Bill that financed the Interstate Highways was none other than Albert Gore Snr, making him indirectly responsible for one of the largest carbon footprints in history – a legacy now addressed by his son.

The sheer scale of the US road system covering its national territory dwarfed other advanced economies even before the Second World War. The widespread motorisation of societies witnessed road construction on a massive scale, especially in Europe. Already before the war, the German autobahn system had been politically envisaged as a direct challenge to the spectre of American economic domination. Indeed the outstanding American road engineer, Thomas Harris Mac-Donald, had spent nearly a year inspecting the Reichsautobahn, including a high level meeting with Hitler, while vaunting the scale and superiority of American road building. The Nazi regime achieved 3,000 kilometres of autobahn before the outbreak of the war, adding only a few hundred more in the war years, well short of the intended 7,000 kilometres. The autobahn system was built in significant part for the Volkswagen. The Nazi ideology was for the creation of a car for the *German* Volk: a popular cheap car affordable to the German working class. It was to be an integral part of the Volksgemeinschaft (racial community) vision, along with a radio, the Volkspropagandaradio, and a range of other Volks products (Shand, 1984). But the Volkswagen itself was a spectacular failure. Having been brought under a forced nationalisation involving Porsche and BMW financing a factory by public funds and supported by consumer subscriptions, not a single Volkswagen was produced for civilian use before the defeat of Nazism (Tooze, 2007).

The main wave of climate change driven by the motorisation of society followed the Second World War, with the rapid acceleration of both road building and car production. And, it was then that, in Germany, the Volkswagen beetle really took to the roads. Worldwide, the annual number of new domestic vehicles increased more than 10 times between 1945 and 2000. But, alongside societally varied road infrastructures there were distinctive national vehicle fleets, often designed by national flagship motor manufacturers. Although now belonging to a previous epoch, the original British mini, the Citroen 2CV, the Italian Fiat 500, drove in parallel national lanes to the German Volkswagen. Although the emergence of a single market in Europe, and the amalgamation and internationalisation of manufacturer ownership, has to an extent globalised societal trends, societal differences remain stark. The unique Brazilian car fleet of Flex Fuel Vehicles was achieved by a political compact between President Lula and the major global car manufacturers. But once more the USA stands at the forefront of distinctive national car fleets on the key climate change dimension of size. In 2017, the average weight of an American car was nearly 30% heavier than the average car on the roads in Germany, and a massive 55% heavier than average cars driven in Japan. Weight of car is the single biggest factor behind the massive difference in per capita petrol consumption in the USA noted above. It is a simple combination of weight x continental road infrastructure x car dependency generating CO_2 at a societally unparalleled level.

For a short time in the USA there was a slight moderation in extravagance of weight and engine power, with the emergence of the 'compact': even that only relatively smaller. But then came the SUV (Sports Utility Vehicle). The fashion for SUVs is a social phenomenon, a climate change tango between producers and consumers, rather than an expression of individual consumer preferences. The SUV craze is a classic example of social contagion by imitation and competition. In the USA, between 2010 and 2019 the SUV share of new car sales rose from 27% to 50%. In Europe, where SUVs are large but not quite as large as the average American SUV, the share rose from 10% to 36%, while in China, it rose from 14% to 44%. The impact of these different but parallel societal tendencies has already been an increase of extra 3.3 million barrels of oil *per day* attributable exclusively to SUVs between 2010 and 2018. The International Energy Authority calculates that if these present trends continue, the greenhouse gas emissions from SUVs would more than offset the reductions in GHG achieved by 150 million fully electric cars (IEA, 2019). Moreover, already, SUVs have contributed a greater additional increase of CO_2 than any sector other than power generation, at 544 million tonnes between 2010 and 2018, a greater increase than that produced even by heavy industry. They are indeed Socially Undesirable Van-dals, pressing the accelerator on the climate emergency.

Just as America is locked-in to a car production-consumption culture of bigness, so in continental Europe a fuel tax regime has created a domestic car fleet dominated by the diesel engine. The change in the character of the car fleet, and hence its distinctive climate change impact, was both rapid and deep. In the space of two decades from 1990, the balance between petrol and diesel consumption shifted from 55% and 45% respectively to 38% and 62%. In France, Germany, Spain and Italy over 70% of all new car purchases were for diesel engines. In one sense, this demonstrates the power of fuel taxation as a political policy to shape car fleets. But, equally it creates a legacy car fleet and a degree of lock in. Originally, the preference for diesel had been to reduce overall fuel demand, as diesel was more economical. From a climate change perspective, it therefore reduces CO_2 emissions. Now, it is recognised that it has a greater impact by increasing both nitrogen oxide emissions and particulate pollution of the atmosphere. There was a further twist to the tale of European diesel fuel dependency, again demonstrating the power of regulatory instruments to create and destroy.

For a brief period from 2004 to 2013, Germany promoted biodiesel as an environmentally beneficial alternative to fossil diesel, reducing tax to zero. For a short period, diesel cars were being driven on 100% biodiesel, increasing consumption from 450,000 tonnes annually in 2004 to 3.26 million tonnes in 2007. A reversal of policy re-imposing taxes then saw the virtual elimination of 100% biodiesel driven cars from 56% in 2007 to a mere 1% in 2013. This brief flirtation with a replacement of a fossil fuel by a biofuel was significant from a sociogenic of climate change perspective both in the power of tax and quota regulation, and in the environmental resource on which it depended. Biodiesel in Germany was overwhelmingly produced from a domestic agricultural crop, rapeseed, hence the transformation of European fields in Spring to seas of yellow (Harvey & Bharucha, 2016).

The virtual demise of biofuel, and the increasing climate change and environmental hazards of fossil diesel, has reinforced the fossil carbon lock-in. In Europe, petrol has replaced diesel as the dominant fuel, reversing the proportions of a decade ago, with nearly 60% of new car registrations in 2019 fuelled with petrol. Together with fossil diesel, fossil fuel lock-in has re-asserted itself, accounting for 90% of all new cars, chargeable electric and hybrid accounting for a mere 8%, in spite of substantial tax incentives in several countries.

Car and hence oil dependency is further shaped societally by the existence of alternative means of transport, notably railway networks. Overall, density of network (kilometres of rail per square kilometre) is relatively high across Europe, although not quite as high as Japan. Within Europe there is considerable variation, with Germany's much vaunted integrated intra- and inter-urban rail and bus network. Germany has by far the highest rail network density (9 kilometres per square kilometre), more than twice even the European average. France stands out for its high speed rail network, followed by

Spain. Nonetheless, there is a general pattern across Europe of shrinkage of networks from their historical peaks, Italy by 31%, France by 32% and Germany by 37%. Way out in front, however is the United Kingdom which saw a 52% reduction in rail network following the so-called Beeching cuts in the 1960s, which were accompanied by an extensive programme of motorway construction. All these shrinkages combined to accelerate the trends to greater and greater motorisation of society both for domestic and commercial transport. In the UK, travel by rail, bus and cycle halved between 1955 and 2005, a decline of 43 billion passenger kilometres, an amount equalled and exceeded by the growth of road vehicle use over the same period (Wootton, 2004).

This acceleration of motorisation coincided with the rapidly emerging exploitation of United Kingdom North Sea oil, making Britain (along with Denmark) exceptional within the EU and only matched by Norway for having a significant, if short-lived, domestic environmental oil resource. For the UK, oil production rose rapidly from near zero in 1970 to 2.7 billion barrels per day in 1980, peaking in 1999 before rapidly declining, until the UK became a net importer again. Thus, the UK is societally distinctive within Europe for the extent of its de-railment, its pattern of motorisation and motorway building, occurring in combination with access to its new environmental resource of North Sea oil.

In the earlier account of the electrification of society, comparisons and contrasts were drawn with power generation and societal resource environments for coal, hydro, gas and oil. This demonstrated the varied societal patterns in the growth and character of greenhouse gas emissions from the process of electrification. Here, a simple contrast between the USA and Europe can be drawn to account for American exceptionalism in car fleet and consumer petrol consumption. The European Union is the biggest global importer of oil, and with those two minor exceptions of the UK and Denmark, most of its 27 members are over 95% dependent on imported oil. Equally significant is the dominance of road transport as a consumer of oil, with 48% share of oil imports, compared with domestic and international air transport of 9%, the next highest consumer of oil for energy. Finally, to complete this characterisation of European Union countries, over recent decades there has been a marked lock-in to Russian oil, now significantly supplemented by oil from Kazakhstan. Putting these two together, they account for 37% of all oil imports, compared with 16% from the Middle East (Iraq and Saudi Arabia), and much lower percentages from all other countries. Rosneft and Lukoil are by far the largest oil major contributors to Europe's motorised transport. Put it another way, many more European cars are driving around oil from Russia than from any other region. Russian oil keeps Europe moving. Conversely, 70% of Russia's oil is imported by the EU. Here, then, is another example of 'opposites attract', a geopolitical trading bond between key resource poor and key resource rich regions. They form a partnership in climate change.

The United States could scarcely be more contrasting in its post-Second World War trajectory of motorisation and oil dependency. Its growth in motorisation before the war had been fuelled by nationally produced oil, and in 1950 well over 90% of cars drove on American oil. By 1970, its production had doubled, but was failing to keep pace with the growth in consumption, and after reaching this interim peak, its production volumes gradually declined. There was much discussion, and scientific research, suggesting the US (and the world) was reaching 'peak oil'. From this period right through to the early 2000s, the US became increasingly dependent on imported oil, especially from Saudi Arabia and the Persian

Gulf. The geopolitics of protecting the American supply of oil, the movement of aircraft carriers, the wars, and the political alliances, can be linked to the expanding dependency of American motorisation on imported oil. By 2006, 60% of American oil consumption was imported, overwhelmingly from the Middle East, followed by Canada. Then came shale oil and fracking. At the start of the fracking boom, the International Energy Association estimated that fracked oil would postpone 'peak oil' by only 15–20 years. Now, the question is no longer one of peak oil, but how to keep it underground, unexploited. The boom has delivered more or less total oil self-sufficiency, returning the USA to the point of departure in the 1950s. The COVID-19 pandemic has unsettled this return, demonstrating the intensely geopolitical character of oil dependency, the power of the OPEC cartel, and Russian political leverage. As demand dropped, so did prices to a level that threatened the commercial survival of American fracked oil. But, a political deal was needed between the three major parties to reduce production and establish a price floor. American oil self-sufficiency has been secured, and has met the massively increased consumption, now standing at 20 million barrels per day, compared with 6.5 billion in 1950. In the USA, motorisation of transport is even more extreme than Europe, with over 65% of total oil production consumed by passenger cars, and, when combined with road freight reaches 85%. International and domestic flight consumes a mere 9% of US oil consumption (EIA, 2020). American oil feeds all of its increasingly obese car fleet, and no doubt also served to pump up President Trump's fantasy of autarkic nationalism. It is a unique historical and societal trajectory of motorisation driving the climate emergency, a sociogenic interaction between a national political economy and its resource environment.

POWERING INTO THE CLIMATE EMERGENCY

This chapter has tracked major transformations of society in their electrification and motorisation. Following the industrial revolution (Chapter 3), these are further major waves of climate change acceleration. A similar analysis could be developed for aviation, how different societies take flight. It might come as no surprise, that small, relatively wealthy islands (Iceland and the Republic of Ireland) have the highest per capita travel by flight, followed by the USA and China, where, given their vast territorial span at the opposite extreme, there are relatively high volumes of domestic flying. The pandemic has brought to attention the reliance of different national airlines on tourist traffic, taking people from environments relatively deprived of sun and beaches to countries which possess them – along with their different cultures of food consumption, social life or architecture. But the main story for burning fossil fuels, and hence for generating the climate emergency, arises overwhelmingly from power generation and road transport, hence the focus of this chapter.

In both cases, the generation of climate change can be understood as historical and societal processes on a grand scale. The scale of the transformations is critical. Strategic and political development of infrastructures, whether of power generation or of road networks, created the condition of possibility for the consumption arising from the use of electricity or roads. The various worlds of consumerism, of domestic electric goods and motor vehicles, expanded in conjunction with the enlargement of infrastructures. This much is shared across different societies. But, whether for power generation and domestic electrical goods or for road networks and motor vehicles, different societies and regions exhibit huge variation, and with consequential differences both in the pace and scale of sociogenic climate change. In the

USA, the consumption of petrol for cars, the size and weight of cars, especially with the social fashion of SUVs, combined with the dominance of road infrastructures, delivers a magnitude of scale greater climate change impact than European or Japanese equivalents. There are significant societal differences in domestic electric equipment, notably air conditioning or refrigeration, toasters or TVs, but even greater variation in the generation of electricity that powers them. These histories demonstrate important variations in cultures of production, market creation, and consumption (PDEC) in different societies, in relation to the resource environments they inhabit.

This analysis also points to a significant difference between electrification and motorisation. For electrification the main source of greenhouse gases, hence the critical political point of intervention, is at the point of production of electricity, rather than the consumer choice and use of domestic electrical equipment. In the case of motorisation, road construction of itself is of much less climate change significance than the burning of oil, hence the consumer choice and use of motor vehicles. In this case, apart from radical changes in alternative infrastructures for mobility, the political point of intervention is located in the end consumer market, the necessary revolution in vehicle design and traction. This sociogenic analysis of climate change indicates that different political points of intervention to prevent and reverse the climate emergency apply.

As with the previous chapter's analysis of food, historical and societal analysis of climate change generation demonstrates the huge challenges to be confronted differently by different societies in reversing the climate emergency. Cultures of production, market formation, and consumption are deeply embedded in people's whole modes of living. One only has to listen to Bob Dylan, for example, to hear ringing in one's ears the emotional commitment to an extravagant road and car culture so threatening to the future of the planet. The 'intelligent house' now interconnects almost all the electrical equipment in domestic life spaces, with a promise of artificial intelligence that will save the last vestiges of human labour and energy. In this chapter, the analysis of societally varied processes of electrification and motorisation has pointed to differences characteristic of different nations or regions irrespective of inequalities of wealth either between or within countries. These inequalities entrench the embeddedness of climate-changing lifestyles on a different plane, only magnifying the challenge of preventing a climate catastrophe. That is the focus of the next chapter.

But these histories also show another face. Strategic political decisions underpinned both electrification and motorisation of societies. In most national cases, whether in building roads or deciding to go nuclear for power generation, these decisions had the urgency of military, national security, or even wartime necessities. In many cases, they were taken in response to a crisis, such as the Great Depression. If strategic political decisions were taken to address these necessities and so unwittingly put the planet on the road to catastrophe, so too can they be taken to address the urgent necessity of reversing climate change. If they are to succeed, however, given that embedded lifestyles are so structured by inequalities, addressing inequalities of wealth and inequalities of access to environmental resources also becomes critical for any future green transformation.

6

INEQUALITIES OF CLIMATE CHANGE

The growth of wealth inequalities between and within nations has historically been, and remains now, the driving force of climate change. The British industrial revolution led the 'great divergence' in wealth between leading economies and the rest of the world and at the same time led the acceleration of greenhouse gas emissions. It was *the* world leader in wealth creation and climate change. Over the past two centuries and more, the defining characteristic of economic growth has been to both feed and fuel climate change.

Moreover, the emergence of industrial capitalism entailed new forms of wealth inequalities *within* nations. The development of capital ownership with joint stock companies and equity markets together with the divergence between top salaries of market traders, bankers, managers or middle class professionals and manual workers, skilled, unskilled and precarious, resulted in social inequalities both novel and extreme. In the contemporary world, the level of inequalities within many societies across the world is higher now than at any stage, even compared with the period immediately prior to the First World War (Piketty, 2014). The previous chapter discussed how different societies generate climate change differently, through electrification and motorisation, putting to one side their internal social inequalities. But, put bluntly, rich people amplify the distinctive climate change characteristics of the societies they inhabit. They lead the forcing of climate change within the countries that lead the forcing of climate change. It is a doubled-up sociogenic climate change impact.

This chapter will explore the range of inequalities that are at the heart of the sociogenic dynamics of climate change. It will do so first by examining how national wealth inequalities are linked to unequal national contributions to climate change. It will then turn to demonstrate how inequalities within different nations also exhibit the same relationship between wealth and greater impact on the earth's atmosphere. Most of the studies on this aspect of societal inequalities focus on consumption, pointing the climate change finger at the extravagances of consumption of the rich. This one-sided emphasis on consumption will be challenged, arguing that inequalities of wealth and income and price hierarchies of goods and services, are dynamically related to inequalities of consumption. This perspective hence ties in together inequalities of wealth, inequalities of consumption and unequal generation of climate change.

However, this relationship between inequalities of market wealth and climate change is one major dimension. Throughout this book, an attempt has been made always to situate political economies in interaction with their varied resource environments, whether in their own national territories, or accessed by conquest or trade (Fig. 1.2). So another dimension concerns the inequalities between different societies in terms of their resource environments: the presence or absence of resources in fossil energy, minerals, sun, rain and fertile land. The significance of these inequalities in resource environments has been signalled at various points in the book already: the USA with its history of energy autarky and land wealth; China rich in coal, poor in agricultural land; the partnership in climate change between Japan and Australia for coal. As has already been demonstrated, these environmental resource inequalities are intimately related to the different trajectories of national economic growth, and hence the different ways they induce climate change. The societal inequalities of wealth generation intersect with societal inequalities of environmental resource to produce distinctive sociogenic processes of climate change.

INEQUALITIES BETWEEN COUNTRIES AND CLIMATE CHANGE

In the 2019 world scientists' second warning of the climate emergency (Ripple, Wolf, Newsome, Barnard, & Moomaw, 2019), they present a table (Supplementary data, Table S1) of the world's most greenhouse generating nations. From their natural scientists' perspective, it seemed obvious to rank the top 26 nations according to which produced the most CO_2 equivalent and which produced the least. China tops the list, followed by the United States, the European Union (taken as a whole), India, Russia and Japan. Australia comes in as the 15th biggest emitter, and Singapore as the 21st. China produces nearly twice as much CO_2 as the United States, and 2.7 times more than the whole of the European Union. Presenting the data in this way could suggest that, from the standpoint of the planetary climate emergency, China is the biggest problem, and, as was discussed in Chapter 1, from the standpoint of impact on the atmosphere, that is clearly the case.

As a general point however, the scientists acknowledge that

> ...*the climate crisis is closely linked to excessive*
> *consumption of the wealthy lifestyle. The most*
> *affluent countries are mainly responsible for the*
> *historical GHG emissions and generally have the*
> *greatest per capita emissions.*

(Ripple et al., 2019)

So, from a sociogenic perspective, the key dynamic here is the relationship between wealth (in terms of per capita Gross Domestic Product) and climate change generation (CO_2 per capita per year). There is a direct correlation between the two, the wealthier the average per capita wealth of a nation, the greater the per capita greenhouse gas emissions (Fig. 6.1). This

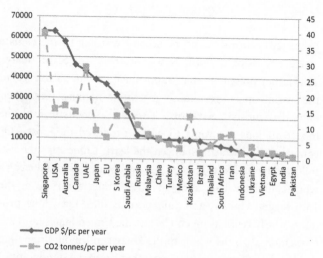

Source: Table S1, World scientists' warning of a climate emergency. *Bioscience*, 4.11.2019.

Fig. 6.1. National Wealth and Climate Change. Countries ranked by per capita GDP, highest (left) to lowest (right) of top 25. GDP in $ pc per year, RH; CO_2 tonnes pc per year, LH.

re-ranks the countries in terms of the generation of GHG rather than the national aggregate GHG impact on the atmosphere. With the outlier exception of the intensely urbanised and energy import dependent Singapore, the USA tops the table, and China drops to twelfth. The average wealth production of a US citizen is six times greater than the average wealth production of a Chinese citizen, and the average US citizen produces two and a half times more CO_2 equivalent than a Chinese citizen. The case of India is even more striking. The average US citizen produces 30 times more wealth than the average Indian, and nine times more CO_2. The European Union, which will be explored in more detail below, has just over half the wealth per citizen of the United States, and less than half the CO_2 per capita.

Looking at the downward curve of the graph of both per capita wealth and per capita CO_2, there are a few blips and dips. These support the central idea of situating political economies in their resource environments: the blips are produced by countries whose wealth derives significantly from oil or coal (United Arab Emirates, Saudi Arabia, Kazakhstan, Iran), and the dip in the case of Brazil, which we have already seen derives little of its energy for electrification or transport from fossil fuels. Saudi Arabia produces three times more CO_2 per dollar of per capita wealth than Brazil. Australia, with its coal resources, also produces a high level of CO_2 per dollar of wealth.

Inequalities within Societies and Climate Change

The inequalities between societies just discussed only give a very rough and ready, if powerful, demonstration of the relation between national wealth production and climate change. The relation between wealth and inequalities becomes much starker, however, if instead the searchlight is directed on the consumption and lifestyles of the wealthiest households and individuals *within* societies. To coincide with the United Nations Cop 21 meeting in Paris in 2015, Oxfam published a report, *Extreme Carbon Inequality*. They demonstrated that the richest 10% of the world's global population contributed 49% of global GHG emissions. By contrast, the poorest 50% of the world's population, around 3.5 billion people, contributed only 10% of global emissions. At the extreme ends of global individual wealth, the richest top 1% of the world's population generated 175 times more climate warming gases than the poorest 10% through the goods and services they purchased and consumed.

Individual wealth inequalities, and the purchasing power they represent, are thus central to any understanding of the societal processes of climate change generation. The stark figures just cited refer to the global rich wherever they are. But it can come as no surprise that the richest countries have the highest number of the world's richest 10%, with the USA out in front with about a third of the global top 10%.

The switch from GDP per capita as a measure of produced wealth to wealth manifest in consumption is decisive in apportioning responsibility for emissions deriving from inequalities. In one sense, it is very simple. People with more purchasing power purchase more. The more they purchase the greater their exploitation of earth's resources, the more energy they use, and the greater the impact they have on the earth's atmosphere. Those with the means can purchase goods produced from across the world and travel with ease and frequency across the world. As consumers their per capita emissions consequently reveal greater levels of inequalities than the per capita emissions of producers from within national territories (Chancel & Piketty, 2015). As we shall later see, this is an important shift in focus. However, it is too simple.

Consumer inequalities within countries for CO_2 emissions are dramatic, and, moreover, it is the richest within the richest countries that are literally consuming the future of the planet. Looking at G20 countries, Oxfam demonstrated that in the USA the top 10% of richest earners' consumption generated 50 tonnes of CO_2 equivalent per capita per year compared with the bottom 40% consumers that generated 13 tonnes CO_2 equivalent per capita per year. But, given the wealth disparities between nations, the top 10% in every other G20 was significantly lower than the top 10% in the USA: the UK's top 10% consumers generated less than half that of the top 10% in the USA per capita, at 24 tonnes CO_2 equivalent per capita per year, with Germany at 14 and France at 13 tonnes CO_2 equivalent per capita per year. Significantly, these differences suggest that the more unequal the society – the USA and UK leading the pack here – the greater the per capita emissions of the top 10%. Just comparing the USA and the UK as two highly unequal societies, the threshold for the top 10% in the USA is \$155,105 per annum compared with £55,000 (approximately \$71,000) for the UK. In other words, the US top 10% has double the purchasing power of the UK top 10%. Although the growth of the middle class and richest people in China has dramatically changed the overall picture of global national inequalities, nonetheless in the latest available figures, the richest top 10% people in China have a carbon footprint through their per capita consumption equivalent to the poorest 40% of Europeans. So, in terms of consumption, 40% of the world's top emitters reside in North America and account for 45% of global emissions, whereas China hosts the largest proportion (35%) of middle range emitters, and India 36% of the world's bottom 50% emitters responsible for just 13% of global emissions (Chancel & Piketty, 2015). And to wrap up this brief sketch of unequal purchasing powers, at its pinnacle, the top 1% of the richest individuals in the USA have been calculated to generate 300 tonnes CO_2 equivalent per capita per year, more than the poorest of the world in a lifetime.

Overall, therefore, the richest consumers within the richest and most unequal nations are responsible for the highest levels of climate warming emissions. They represent the historical legacy of the 'great divergence', now being progressively modified rapidly by China, and much less so by Russia, India and Brazil. Dollars translate into emissions through lifestyles, whether of the ultra-rich or the poor and precarious. The top 1% of Americans just referred to typically might travel between New York and Los Angeles five times a year, or fly twice a year or more to Europe or elsewhere. As of 2016, there were 12,717 registered private jets in the USA, compared with 435 in Germany, or 345 in the UK. China has the most rapid growth in private jet ownership, but with a grand total of 277 registered. But, as we observed in the previous chapter, consumption of aviation fuel per capita pales into insignificance when compared with the fuel consumption of private road vehicles.

When considering how greenhouse gases are generated by the purchasing power of the rich, or, for that matter of the poor, the whole fabric of their lifestyles, the whole bundle of their social life practices consuming energy, housing, food and materials, has to be considered. The sociogenesis of climate change is much more than an equation between purchasing power in dollars and tonnes CO_2 equivalent per capita per year. The challenge of the climate emergency arises from how purchasing power, rich or poor, is deeply embedded in the routines and patterns of social lives.

In the most general terms, the consumption of petrol for domestic cars and gas and electric energy for heating, lighting and cooking in the home exhibit massive differences between the top 10% rich and the bottom 10%. A survey of 86 countries found that the top 10% consumed 187 times more vehicle fuel and 13 times more heating and electricity for the home (Oswald, Owen, & Steinberger, 2020). More detailed data on the USA show a very similar pattern. In the previous chapter it was noted that the average American consumes 4 to 5 times more petrol for domestic cars than the average European. Turning to the richest of the rich within the USA, they consume a very similar multiple more than the bottom decile of American consumers. Although the budgets of the poorest concentrate on the 'necessities' of food, heating, driving, it is nonetheless a remarkable feature of the top 10% that vehicle petrol and domestic utilities of gas and electricity account for well over half of the greenhouse gas generated by their expenditure on consumer goods. So although the rich generate greenhouse gases from a much wider range of goods and services than the poor, on clothing, communications, and recreation, nonetheless petrol and household energy still dominate their carbon footprints but on a hugely greater scale. Moreover, there is a distinctive spatial aspect to this greenhouse gas generating consumption of the rich. The highest levels of consumer fossil energy use are found in wealthy suburbs with the lowest population densities, with more driving and larger houses reflecting a radically different lifestyle from inner city apartment blocks inhabited by the bottom 10% (Ummel, 2014). Put crudely, being rich can buy you more space, or in the city centre, the privileged space of a penthouse. And, if very rich, both. A very similar pattern was found in the 'prospering suburbs' of the United Kingdom, where vehicle use, flying and domestic energy use remain responsible for producing almost 50% of these rich consumers' GHG footprint, in spite of their purchasing of a much wider range of goods and services than those with less purchasing power (Druckman & Jackson, 2009).

As we have already seen, the consumption of the Chinese richest top 10% equates with the bottom US 40%. The consumption lifestyles of the rapidly growing middle classes and urban elites in China also dominate the greenhouse gases generated from vehicle use and domestic energy. Here the top 40% consume 78% of all vehicle fuel, while the bottom 30% consume only 7%. Although patterns of inequality are very different from the USA, nonetheless the relative purchasing power of the rich is expressed in larger vehicles consuming more petrol, and the greater domestic comforts of central heating, air-conditioning and electrical equipment (Wiedenhofer et al., 2017).

The simple logic of greater purchasing power resulting in more goods and services purchased, leading to greater CO_2 emissions of the richest within the richest societies is a powerful representation of the inequalities in responsibilities for the climate emergency. Societal greenhouse gas emissions may culminate in consumption, as the end point where statistics can conveniently capture how purchasing power converts into greenhouse gases. But purchasing power and consumption embrace far from the whole story of the societal inequalities driving climate change. There is a risk of responsibilising the consumer as the sole or primary agent driving climate change, with a moralising politics exhorting individual behaviour change.

Inequalities in purchasing power and the production of the whole range of goods (houses, cars, food, clothing, etc.) from luxury high price to low price basic essentials, are the necessary preconditions for the actual purchase and consumption end-use of these goods and services. But inequalities in purchasing power cannot just be the taken-for-granted starting point for analysing climate change generation. Consumption is only a phase in a continuous circular process with production and market exchange (Harvey, 2007; Harvey &

Geras, 2018). In addition to the wealth inequalities derived from capital ownership, inequalities of purchasing power are created in labour markets and within the wage hierarchies internal to firms. Larger firms, particularly those with monopoly or near-monopoly power within markets, exhibit the widest spread of purchasing power inequalities within their labour forces, directly or indirectly employed by them. This is especially a feature of global corporations where the highest salaries are found in the headquarters, the lowest in the peripheries of their supply chains, nationally and internationally. Even within a couple of years of the 2007–2008 great crash, a Chief Executive Officer of a major US company typically earned 243 times the income of the average employee. There is of course, enormous variation in the stretch of wage, salary and bonus reward systems between countries, depending on the legal organisation of labour markets, the power of trades unions, or the significance of ethnic minority and gender divisions. If there is stretch at the top, there is also stretch at the bottom with the epidemic of zero hours contracts and bogus or precarious self-employment. The stretch has also infected the public sector, with top managers – such as Vice Chancellors within UK universities – being paid 30 times the pay of a manual worker within their organisations. To put that another way, they earn more in one year than the manual worker does in a lifetime of 30 years of work. Celebrity pay, whether in sports or entertainment, reaches stratospheric levels in leading economies, without damaging, but possibly even enhancing, the profit-making capacities of the organisations that engage them.

There is a yet deeper connection between inequalities of purchasing power, the consumer and the generation of climate change. One of the key characteristics of profit-making enterprises is to create quality distinction in the goods and services they deliver to the market (Harvey & Geras, 2018).

Quality distinction aims at avoiding competition between, and comparison of, like for like products and services. The aim is to be unlike, different and unique, whether in the quality of good and service, the quality of the shopping experience, the complexity of financial packaging wrapped up with the purchase, or a combination of all of the above encapsulated in market branding. There is competition to avoid competition, to achieve a quasi-monopoly position in the market. Nowhere is this more evident than the branding and distinction of luxury goods and services, from houses, to cars, domestic equipment, clothes, food, hairstyles, tax management or legal advice. Quality distinction is at the pinnacle in the niche markets for those endowed with highest purchasing power. The whole bundle of quality distinctive goods and services constitute the quality distinction of the lifestyles of those with greatest purchasing power. Marks of distinction also make their own carbon footprint: the Rolls Royces of climate change. The luxury car or house requires more fossil energy both in its making and in its using. The generation of unequal purchasing power and hierarchies of income and wealth are inherently connected to hierarchies and distinctions in quality and price of goods and services. These hierarchies of inequality in production and market structure then culminate in the consumer purchases and end-use of goods and services that generate the huge inequalities of greenhouse gas emissions of the top 10% discussed above. There is a continuous circular process connecting production, to exchange and consumption (the PDEC again), so generating climate change. The impact of consumers and their role in generating climate change can only be understood within this wider framing of production-exchange-consumption economic organisation.

Within this cycle, the consumer plays a critical role in ensuring the loop of inequality and profitability is unbroken. Far from the myth of the sovereign power of the consumer, the individual exercise of choice in the market, whether as a poor or rich consumer, is always that of the price taker rather than price maker. Consumers do not set prices in modern markets as a consequence of their individual choices. The creation of market power through the monopolisation of an Amazon, Microsoft, or Facebook, or the quasi-market monopolies of the dominant retailers and manufactures with the anti-competitive market positioning leaves consumers systemically paying the price of profit. Consumers never know the profit margins of the goods or services they purchase, or the costs of production. In the asymmetries of power between producers and consumers, the consumer is always 'sucking the fuzzy end of the lollipop' (Marilyn Monroe, in Some Like It Hot). The capitalist owners of an enterprise give with one hand to the top and bottom of their wage hierarchies what they take back with the other in the luxury niche market or the discount store (Harvey & Geras, 2018). The loop is closed.

Furthermore, as we saw in the previous chapter, the societal generation of greenhouse gases is fundamentally conditioned by the infrastructures of consumption, the generation of electricity and the construction of alternative mobility infrastructures, roads, rail and airports. The state has historically been, and remains, a key agent in creating the conditions of possibility for the lifestyles of consumption, for those with high or low purchasing power. Consumers do not choose, when they buy an SUV, what kind of energy was used in its manufacture any more than does the manufacturer. Nor does the consumer as consumer directly choose the road system on which they drive, or the kind of electricity (coal, gas, hydro, nuclear) used for domestic electrical equipment. In the United Kingdom, it was a political choice, rather than a consumer one, to switch from coal gas to natural gas for domestic heating and cooking. So, although

the inequalities of purchasing power expressed in the purchase of consumer goods captures the final consequence of
consumers' market purchases for inequalities of greenhouse
gas emissions, how, how much, and what fossil energy is
emitted is fundamentally conditioned by the political choices
of national governments.

Finally, to conclude this section on the importance of
wealth inequalities (both market and public wealth) and
climate change generation, the inequalities of consumption
within nations are themselves dependent on the historical
economic growth of those nations. The fact that the purchasing power of the top 10% of the US consumer begins at
twice the purchasing power of the equivalent UK consumer,
or that the per capita purchasing power of the top 10%
of Chinese consumers is equivalent to the per capita
purchasing power of the bottom 40% of European consumers, reflects the outcome of the divergent historical
economic growth of nations. It makes all the difference of
being in the top 10% of the richest nation, as against being
in a less economically powerful economy, both in terms of
purchasing power and of consequent greenhouse gas emissions. As argued in previous chapters, the 'great divergence',
first of the United Kingdom, followed by Northern Europe
and the USA, created inequalities of national wealth on an
unprecedented historical scale. Inequalities of consumer
purchasing power are within inequalities of national
wealth. These were fossil-fuelled and food-fed trajectories of
unequal economic growth.

The political consequences of this analysis will be more
fully explored in the final chapter. Climate change cannot be
solved just by depriving the billionaire consumers of their
billions, if only because it is surely unthinkable that preserving
the bottom 10% in poverty and precarity is a way of reducing
greenhouse gas emissions. The inequalities go all the way

down both in income scales and GHG emissions. The issue is one of the historical nature of growth, whether of the various industrial capitalisms, Soviet political economies, post-Soviet economies or contemporary market socialisms. They have their distinctive linked characteristics both of generating inequalities and climate change, a constant theme running through this book. The scale and pace of a green transformation of whole societal modes of economic organisation necessary to address the climate emergency requires a radical transformation of the polities of economies in their interactions with resource environments.

Inequalities in Command over Planetary Resources

Inequalities of wealth between and within nations are intimately connected to inequalities in a nation's command over the environmental resources of fossil energy and agricultural land, either in its own national territory or beyond. The British industrial revolution exploited its distinctive coal resources, acquired sugar calories for metropolitan consumption from slave and indentured labour colonial plantations, and commanded the cotton from the American slave economy through its banks and merchant capital. The United States prospered from land acquisition through settler colonialism and benefitted from fossil energy autarky with its own oil and coal resources, except for an interlude of dependency on Middle Eastern oil following the Second World War. Japan developed its own nuclear power industry, supplemented and then increasingly displaced by a symbiotic growth as the dominant importer of Australian coal. In the contrasting national historical trajectories analysed in this book, each is marked by a pattern of economic growth fuelled by fossil energy and land extensification.

In the twentieth century, two world wars demonstrated the strategic significance of national territorial command over environmental resources. The First World War threatened British food supplies and triggered a major policy change with respect to national food security in the post war period. In the Second World War, Germany developed aircraft fuel and synthetic rubber from hydrogenising its own national coal resources, but, faced with critical scarcities and a prolonged war with Britain and the United States, invaded Soviet Russia to acquire access to the Ukraine for food and the Caucasus for oil.

The climate emergency challenges this whole pattern of economic growth, and the national strategic relations of political economies to their environmental resources of fossil energy and agricultural land. It forces us to rethink the relationship between economies and their resource environments, to place economies in their resource environments. What historically have been the key environmental assets underpinning the inequalities of national economic wealth now have to become frozen to prevent global warming. The normalised expanding exploitation of fossil energy and fertile land has to be abandoned. Carbon lock-in has to be replaced by carbon lock-down and agricultural land expansion by agricultural land-limiting. President Trump's championing of a national coal industry or President Bolsonaro's reckless appropriation of the Amazon forest and Cerrado are expressions of an obsolete mentality belonging to a previous epoch.

This shift in perspective towards political economies and their resource environments, and especially the unequal distribution of fossil energy and agricultural land, presents a huge challenge to climate change mitigation. When setting the target of limiting global warming to 2°C, a calculation was made as to what limits there would have to be for consuming fossil energy. It was called a 'carbon budget', and to meet its global warming target, that required imposing a cap on CO_2 emissions of between 870 and 1,240 Giga tonnes. In effect, by fixing this cap, it required environmental resources of oil, gas and coal to remain unexploited, 'un-burned'. The implications are quite dramatic. A third of all economically exploitable oil reserves, half of gas reserves and over 80% of all coal reserves would have to be frozen (McGlade & Ekins, 2015). What had once been major sources of national economic wealth and growth have become environmentally taboo. Moreover, these estimates were made before the IPCC revised its target for global warming to 1.5°C, and cut the global 'carbon budget' to 580 Giga tonnes of CO_2 from consuming fossil energy. To meet that target, even more stringent limits to exploitation of fossil energy reserves are required.

The environmental limits on coal exploitation are both by far the most restrictive and the most challenging. As we have already seen (Chapter 5), there are massive contrasts between nations on the availability of coal reserves and their exploitation for power generation. China is the globally dominant coal producer by a huge margin, accounting for 47% of global production in 2019, with India the next highest at a mere 10% (International Energy Authority, World Energy Statistics). The USA has by far the largest coal reserves (23% of global reserves), followed by the Russian Federation (15%), Australia (14%) and China (13%). Whereas the United States is far less coal dependent for its overall energy generation, China is one of the most dependent on its own national coal resources. Even during these pandemic times, it is adding new coal fired power stations and, in contrast to the rest of the world, growing its coal production by 1.5% per year. Thus, for the world to meet the current IPCC global warming targets, the United States and the Former Soviet Union would each be required to leave well over 200 billion tonnes of coal underground, with China and India locking-down over 100 billion tonnes each. Given their coal dependence, China and India face a starkly unequal loss of potential wealth and energy compared with other nations. For the Japan-Australia couple, their mutual asymmetric reliance presents a similarly distinctive joint loss.

Although the requirement for lock-down of oil is far less restrictive than coal, leaving well over 50% of all reserves unexploited remains a huge climate change mitigation challenge, again falling on those nations most oil dependent for their wealth. The Middle East, with nearly half of all global oil and gas reserves, would take the major hit with a lock-down of 260 billion of barrels unexploited, around 40% of its total oil reserves. Central and South America, with Venezuela having 18% of total global oil reserves, would have to sacrifice well over 40% of its potential oil wealth.

Interlocked Inequalities

Despite the Paris Agreement at the COP21 meeting and national plans addressing climate change mitigation, the addiction to fossil fuel and land extensification economic growth continues inexorably. There is no slow down, let alone reduction. In 2019 China led the growth in coal consumption, the USA led in the growth of oil production and consumption, Russia and the US led the growth in liquid gas production and exports, China and the United Kingdom stand at the top of liquid gas imports (BP Statistical Review of Energy, 2020). The United Nations Emissions Gap report 2019 notes the failure to restrain the growth of CO_2 emissions. New coal fields are developed in Australia, with coal fired power stations in Germany and China under construction. China has been expanding its command over Brazilian soya-growing land, pushing the commodity frontiers.

From the natural science perspective of the aggregate impact of human activity on the earth's atmosphere, it might not matter whether greenhouse gases are produced by the 1,289 global billionaires, the millions in the top 10% of rich people or the billions of very poor people. But, we have come a long way from anthropogenic climate change when accounting for the dynamics of greenhouse gas generation. The previous chapter analysed the societal differences in the sociogenesis of climate change through power generation and terrestrial transport. In this chapter, the different historical trajectories of economic growth fuelled by fossil energy are characterised by a double inequalities lock-in: wealth inequalities within and between nations generated by unequal command over national territorial and traded environmental resources. Greenhouse gases, the forcing of global warming, are the consequence of the interlocking of these double societal inequalities. Climate change is induced by these different unequal historical trajectories. National political economies are deeply embedded in the environmental resources they command. The unequal lifestyles of rich and poor, between and within national political economies, routinize and normalise the huge differences in who generates most CO_2 how and where. The climate emergency is not just an accident of history, but woven into how our societies have become economically and environmentally organised over time and in space. The double inequalities lock us in to a logic of catastrophic climate change. So, unlocking the politico-economic organisations with their unequal command over environmental resources is central to the radical societal transformations necessary to escape from the climate emergency.

7

INTO AND OUT OF(???) THE CLIMATE EMERGENCY

Societies of their own accord start, regulate and
control the material interactions between themselves
and nature. They oppose themselves to Nature as one
of its forces, setting in motion soyabeans and cattle,
cars and planes, light bulbs and boilers, using their
social powers of knowledge in order to appropriate
Nature's productions in a form adapted to their own
demands. By thus acting on the external world and
changing it, societies at the same time change their
own nature. And so they create the climate
emergency.

Adapted from Marx, K. *Capital* Volume 1, p. 177[1]

---

1 The original: 'Man of his own accord starts, regulates, and controls the material re-actions between himself and Nature. He opposes himself to Nature as one of her own forces, setting in motion arms and legs, head and hands, the natural forces of his body, in order to appropriate Nature's productions in a form adapted to his own wants. By thus acting on the external world and changing it, he at the same time changes his own nature'.

The climate emergency requires us to rethink what we mean by societies, their economies, cultures, and polities. It calls on us to rewrite societal histories, from the dawn of civilisation to the present, in a radically different perspective. Nature and the environment cannot be put to one side, bracketed off, left to natural sciences. A new historical materialism fashioned in and by the present, buffeted by hurricanes and fires, melting glaciers and pandemics, needs to emerge.

Sociogenesis of climate change is the central concept which has been developed over the course of this book, both in dialogue with theoretical debates and in a re-viewing of major historical transformations. This is not a global history of climate change. Rather, key moments have been picked out and analysed both to grasp their significance for climate change, and to flesh out the different dimensions of the concept of sociogenesis. The British industrial revolution, American settler colonisation of the continent, the growth of meat production and consumption in China and Brazil, the electrification and motorisation of societies, have served to ground the concept of sociogenesis in particular and historical interactions between societies and their resource environments.

The decisive conceptual move was to plant societies and their economies firmly in the resource environments over which they have command, notably, but by no means exclusively, their immediate national territorial resources. Graphically, the shift from the Fig. 1.1 to 1.2 (Chapter 1, p. 21) is a shift from thinking about societies and their histories outside of any natural environments, to thinking about societies as fundamentally conditioned by the environmental resources they inhabit. To nail down the concept of sociogenesis of climate change, particular interactions between societies and their resource environments are especially significant for generating greenhouse gases: changes in land use with the emergence of agricultures; use of fossil resources for energy and heat.

Planting societies in their resource environments helps to explain how and why different societies grow differently. Rather than think in terms of abstract and universal models of societal economies, societal environmental resources can be seen as a major source of historical variation between societies. Societal variation in space and time is critical for a sociogenic explanation of climate change. In our account of the British industrial revolution, it was not capitalism in general that brought about 'the great divergence' in economic growth and wealth between countries, but a politically instituted economy making critical use of its land and fossil energy resources that distinguished it both from the rest of Europe and from North America for many decades.

The analysis argued that its industrial revolution was based on the combination of England's distinctive coal resources with direct control over slave colonies for producing sugar and calories for the urban proletariat, and the indirect control over slave cotton plantations in the American Deep South. The climate change impact was generated by the conjunction between land clearance and slave agriculture in the New World and the burning of fossil fuels in the metropolis of British industrial capital. The Lancashire textile mills were wedded to the expansion of slave cotton and vice versa. For the central decades of the nineteenth century, Britain burnt 10 times more coal per capita than its European competitors *and* commanded 70% of the US slave cotton crop. The diminutive British land base, which had earlier fostered the explosion of woollen textile production, could never have achieved the industrial take-off with cotton textiles without its counterpart command over the land in the Deep South. That was a connection at the core of the great acceleration in climate change.

But it was more profound than that. Climate change became embedded in a radical transformation of ways of life in Britain, Europe and across the world. Working class wages, as well as the salaries of the rich, were purchasing, wearing, repairing and washing cotton textiles, diminishing the dependence on wool, linen, and leather, or rather, adding a whole new range of qualitative variety. Britain drove a radical re-clothing and adornment of human bodies. Climate change generation was stitched into the very fabric of life. Throughout the analysis, to grasp sociogenesis we need to follow through from production, exchange, and distribution to consumption.

If the British industrial revolution represents a distinctive historical trajectory and processes of generating a combination of greenhouse gases, the nascent United States in the early and central decades of the nineteenth century stands in sharp contrast. Viewed through the lens of climate change, it exhibited a no less significant warming acceleration of the planet's atmosphere. In the natural scientists' Long View of climate change, the transition from hunter-gather societies to settled agriculturalists initiated a much more gradual but under-recognised rise in the level of greenhouses gases. The cultivation of rice from around 3000BC released methane, detected in ice cores as the traces of a major social and economic transformation. Rice cultivation was followed both by the hybridisation and cultivation of other grain crops, and as significant, by the domestication of livestock, sheep, cattle, horses. The slow and steady spread of agriculture and a population dependent on it was only interrupted by the great pandemic of the Black Death, resulting in the retreat of agriculture, reforestation, and the consequent cooling of the earth's atmosphere during the Little Ice Age from the fifteenth to the nineteenth century. But, already before the first great acceleration of the British industrial revolution, agriculture and land-use change had raised the level of greenhouse gases. That was a slow and gradual change occurring across Asia and Europe over millennia.

The territorial expansion of the United States transformed the land-use of the whole continent of North America in a matter of a few short decades. It was a unique climate changing event. The genocides and ethnic cleansing of Native Americans, with their hunter-gatherer and subsistence agricultures, was rapidly displaced by commercial market-oriented agriculture producing the corn, cotton, pigs and cattle of settler colonialism and slave plantations. The incorporation of Texas into the United States in 1845, acquired by force of arms in Mexican and Indian wars, was paradigmatic of the emergent society and economy acquiring huge new land resources. From the time of the Louisiana Purchase in 1803, which at a stroke more than doubled the formal territorial property rights of American white colonists over the heads of indigenous peoples, the United States grew by the forced appropriation of environmental resources on which its economic and social development rested. The Texas longhorn cattle became a major agricultural industry, with the cattle trails celebrated in Western movies. Cattle had already been a European invasive species into the Americas, but Western cowboy expansionism drove this climate changing intrusion to a new level. Hundreds of thousands of cattle converged on Chicago, which, by the 1860s boasted to be 'the bovine capital of the world'. A uniquely American coupling between cattle trails and railways was forged at railheads such as Abilene. It was a marriage of methane producing cattle and fossil fuelled railways of iron and steam locomotives. By the later decades of the nineteenth century, the infamous stockyards of Chicago were supplying chilled beef, transported in specially designed railway wagons, to the East coast cities. Again, the sociogenic analysis goes from production in Texas, distribution in Chicago through to final market exchanges and consumption in New York – and elsewhere. This historical transformation, so typical of ranching societies, was also the formation of the now notoriously American meat-eating consumption culture, with the highest level of meat per capita in the world, reaching 'peak beef' in the 1970s. This is climate change with an American signature.

Each in their distinctive ways, these two historical trajectories contributed to the first great acceleration of climate change. They demonstrate the significance of resource environments and their location in determining the contrasts both in socio-economic development and in how greenhouse gases were generated. The island of Britain and its external colonies versus the progressive appropriation of a continent could scarcely be more consequential for their long-term historical trajectories. To be sure, British merchant capital and its industrial lead secured a dominance over the land-resources of the Deep South cotton plantations. But that too was an aspect of societal variation in the generation of climate change.

Two further waves of climate change acceleration exhibited equally striking societal variation. How different societies were 'electrified', using which environmental resources (coal, oil, gas, hydro), was critical for how and to what extent they generated greenhouse gases. Equally, how societies developed the infrastructures for terrestrial mobility, especially following the Second World War, the building of autobahns, the interstate highway system, or motorways, was critical in providing the conditions for the rapid growth in car ownership and road freight. In Europe, all major nations 'de-railed' to a greater or lesser extent whilst building roads, so directly contributing to the acceleration of climate change.

In both these waves, the state and politically strategic decisions over the shaping of the economy and ensuring energy and national security were principal drivers of sociogenic climate change. When Lenin proclaimed that communism was Soviet power plus the electrification of the whole country, he initiated the first historical example of a central command economic plan for constructing electricity grids. The plan was ambitiously designed to incorporate a centralised system dominated by mega-dams for hydroelectric power. Political struggles and technological constraints, but above all securing access to the Donetsk coal fields and the Baku oilfields, gradually shifted reliance for the electrification of both industry and domestic households onto fossil fuel. This Soviet template of electrification energy stamped its mark on the future of power generation, and hence the characteristic of the intense industrialisation under Stalin for climate change. The political and military control over those particular fossil energy resources, through the Second World War to the present, has remained a source of conflict which only demonstrates the importance of territorial control over environmental resources.

In this time when Green New Deals are being advanced, the symbolic example of the Tennessee Valley Authority (TVA) provides a salutary tale both of the exercise of state power and of the imposing presence of environmental resources. At its initiation, the TVA was strategically developed both to enhance the electrification of society and to lift the economy out of the Great Depression. Benefitting from the volume and fall of the Tennessee River, from our current retro-perspective the massive TVA dams were also providing power from green rather than fossil environmental resources. But that was not the end of the story. Driven in part by the need for energy for the aluminium industry that was fulfilling an imperative of manufacturing military planes, the TVA built a coal-fired power station relying on the conveniently situated Appalachian coalfields. By the mid-1970s coal-powered electricity generation outstripped the hydro-capacity by five times, and the Philadelphia Electricity Company had become the largest coal consumer in the world.

The New Deal prospect of energy generation had turned decisively from green to black. The spatial proximity of river and coal resources conditioned the politically strategic decisions for the provision of electricity.

If these early Soviet and American examples serve to demonstrate how variation in national resource environments condition how climate change is generated for the electrification of societies, the contemporary differences between nations in how they generate power exhibit similar strategic political responses to their access to, or command over, resource environments. France and Brazil stand out for their substantial independence from fossil fuel resources, the first because of its shift into nuclear power in response to a relative lack of national coal resources and the Middle East oil crisis of the 1970s, the second because of its exploitation of hydropower from its major river systems. Brazil depends on fossil energy for less than a quarter of its power generation, France for less than 6%. At the opposite extreme, Poland, China and India stand out for having 70–80% reliance on coal, while Saudi Arabia 'naturally' depends on oil and gas.

These huge societal variations in energy resource environments and consequent production of power for industrial and domestic electrification translates into the consumption of electricity in the domestic household. Even Lenin's vision of electrification in the early 1920s spoke of the liberation of 'domestic slaves' from the household toils of heating and lighting as a primary benefit of electrical supply. The interwar new industries for household domestic equipment, with often a female assembly line workforce replacing domestic servants, produced an array of household equipment: vacuum cleaners, kettles, toasters, cookers, washing machines, eventually microwaves and dishwashers, along with an ever expanding range of household leisure goods and computers. Sociogenically, one of the huge societal

variations in consumption of electricity arises from a combination of climate and wealth. There are more than one air-
conditioning unit per capita for every household in the USA,
as against one per household in 40% of Chinese households
and only 10% of European households. The USA accounts
for over half the total global energy-use for cooling in work-
places. The quadrupling of air-conditioning units since the
1990s appears like a Sisyphean race against time to cope
with global warming by accelerating it.

Consumers as consumers in different societies do not
choose, in general, how the electricity they consume is produced. We plug in to politically determined infrastructures.
Given the scale of investment in national or regional grids,
when we plug in we are also locked-in to whatever the character of the electricity, positive or negative, for climate change.
As we have seen, wealth inequalities between and within
nations have a major significance for how much electricity
households consume. But when we plug in, we are also locked-
in to a whole array of social life reliant on the use of domestic
electric equipment, from waking to sleeping, from eating to
entertaining, from heating to refrigerating, from cleaning to
home-working. We are live-wired. Whereas we have seen that
there are significant examples of how to escape or intensify a
carbon-intensive lock-in for the production of electricity, it is
difficult to imagine a social life un-plugged. Indeed, climate
change mitigation policies, if anything, suggest an intensification of electrification, with the replacement of gas, coal or oil
energy for domestic heating and cooking. Whereas there is
scope for enhancing domestic electrical energy efficiency,
including in the technologies of domestic equipment, social
lives in societally varying ways and extents, are locked-in
to being electrically empowered. That presents a particular
political challenge, rather than consumer challenge, to
addressing the climate emergency.

'Cars made America', or so Bob Dylan celebrated in song. Space and oil are the key aspects of a society's resource environment within which major political decisions under-pinning the motorisation of society rest: the construction of road versus rail systems, the organisation of urban and sub-urban spaces, the strategic fostering of national motor man-ufacturers with their distinctive styles. The abundance of space and, with the exception of a few decades following the Second World War, self-sufficiency in oil was an environ-mental resource context which has placed the United States in a league of its own for a motorised society. The characteristic size and weight of the American domestic car fleet and the social reliance on vehicular transport is expressed in the fact that the average American burns between four and five times more petrol than the average European. Maintaining the 30% size difference between American and other national car fleets, the social fashion for SUVs has resulted in the single most rapid acceleration of greenhouse gas emissions other than the use of fossil fuel for power generation, more than the growth in energy burnt by industry. There are around 50% more cars per 1,000 people in the USA than in any European country, and four times more per capita than in China, even though China now has the biggest car fleet in the world with 360 million vehicles. In weighing the significance for climate change of an America made by the car, it should be recognised that domestic cars account for 65% of US oil consumption, with a further 20% for road freight. In spite of relatively high level of domestic flying, only 9% of their oil is consumed by Americans flying domestically and internationally. Road and rail infrastructures are societal features for organizing social connectivity and mobility, and as such a major aspect of societal variation. Whereas rail and public transport have always been subordinate features of America, the major growth of motorway systems in European countries coincided with their regressive 'de-railment', most notably in the United Kingdom with cuts of over 50% to the rail network in the 1960s. As with electric power generation, consumers do not, as consumers, choose the transport infrastructures which promote how they drive what cars where.

Electrification and motorisation form the skeletal structures of society, the grids and the road networks through which social life flows, and hence how social life generates climate change. They exemplify the political and economic interactions of societies with their resource environments lying behind these two major accelerations of greenhouse gases inducing global warming. In developing the concept of sociogenesis, these examples not only again demonstrate the hugely contrasting variations between societies, but now also highlight the role of different political systems and the political role of states in generating climate change. Then, as citizens and consumers, we are locked-in to infrastructures that penetrate and recast the shape of the shared social practices that constitute social life.

National territorial resource environments are unquestionably significant for the variation between nations in their climate-changing historical trajectories. By the same token inequalities, including the absence of key environmental resources, are the flip-side of that coin. The fact that the USA and Brazil have largely developed with energy and food self-sufficiency provides a platform both for populist nationalism and for rejection of international accords on climate change, never mind climate change denial. But, in many ways, they are the exceptions. This book has highlighted both presence and absences in national territorial resource environments: in agricultural land, in oil and coal.

Three examples have been picked out to illustrate this dimension of sociogenesis. China stands out for its addictive dependence on its own national territorial coal for power generation. But it also stands out for the lack of enough high quality agricultural land to ensure food security, let alone enhancement of standards of diet or the transition to eating more meat. For decades after the Chinese Revolution, food self-sufficiency had dominated the politics of agriculture. It drove another climate changing transformation of Chinese agriculture, the industrial development of its own nitrogen phosphate fertilizer, and subsequently its subsidised excessive use. China became the largest single user of chemical fertilizers, and its wasteful adoption resulted in their becoming a significant element of China's overall greenhouse gas emissions. But, first enhancing and then destroying the productive capacity of land, in 2001, China realised that given its limited land and water resources, it had to abandon food self-sufficiency. Following Europe, China became the largest importer of soyabeans from Brazil, essentially for feeding its rapidly expanding pork production. Brazil, by contrast, had become the agricultural powerhouse of the world, at the expense of pushing the commodity frontiers into the Amazon and Mato Grasso. It was a case of opposites attract: China's lack of land and water tango-ing with Brazil's abundance. This relationship then became Brazil's major distinction for climate change generation, especially with the advent of increasing beef exports to China. Having reacted to its relative although not total lack of petrol resources, Brazil developed biofuels both from cane and soya, so reducing its use of fossil fuel energy. But, as a consequence its livestock and agricultural production now produce over *20 times* more CO_2 equivalent than the whole of its power generation and industry. Not China on its own, nor Brazil on its own, but the marriage between China's lack of food self-sufficiency and Brazil's abundance of land, water and sun has become a sociogenic forcing dynamic of climate change. The devastation of Amazonian rainforest and cerrado biomes, so critical for the future of the planet, were the outcome of these geo-political forces. The fateful combination of Trump and Bolsonaro was seen to intensify this devastation in the perfect mega-storm for climate change in the Amazon.

Yet more briefly summarised here, Japan and Australia have similarly consolidated a partnership in climate change. Following the Fukushima nuclear power disaster, Japan dramatically increased its dependence on Australian coal, lacking fossil energy resources itself. Although, as we have seen, Australia stands out for the dominance of coal for its own power generation, it exports 70% of its total coal production, and Japan imports almost half of Australia's total exports. They are wedded together in sociogenically forcing climate change.

A similar absence and presence has increasingly drawn the European Union into energy dependency on Russia. In a parallel to Japan, Germany's decision to phase out nuclear power has led to increased dependency on coal and especially gas from Russia, with the Nord Stream 2 pipeline project symbolising the prospective umbilical cord binding them together. Although much more below the radar, a similar shift has occurred for increasing dependency on Russian petrol imports for transport, overtaking dependency on Middle East oil. Over a third of petrol consumption by EU domestic car fleets is now Russian, with Rosneft and Lukoil the largest oil companies providing for Europe's motorised transport. Conversely, 70% of Russia's oil exports go to the EU. There is a powerful co-dependency in climate change between Russia and the EU, even if it doesn't quite make a monogamous marriage.

These three examples demonstrate the critical role of international trade in generating climate change, linking producers with consumers. There is a narrative of globalisation that suggests that everything seamlessly goes everywhere in globally integrated markets. Even in financial markets, that is far from being the case. But much trade, as these examples clearly show, is highly structured in relation to absences and presences of environmental resources. In developing the concept of sociogenesis, these absences and presences, and consequent trade flows, expand the understanding of how different political economies interact with resource environments to produce climate change.

Moreover, this takes us straight into a further major contribution of the sociogenic concept: the generation of inequalities as an integral aspect of the generation of climate change. The 'great divergence' in the wealth of industrialising nations from the rest of the world was at one and the same time a great divergence in which nations were responsible for the acceleration of climate change. Moreover, the process of national wealth creation was in significant part the process of generating the greenhouse gases that impacted on the earth's atmosphere. And last but not least, new inequalities *within* nations in societally varied ways and to different extremes provided the richer strata in society with greater purchasing power over earth's resources. So the richest within the richest nations consumed the products that have been and are responsible for climate change on a greater scale than anyone else in the world: houses, cars, clothes, domestic equipment and so on.

The concept of sociogenesis of climate change thus binds the societal interactions of political economies and their resource environments together with the generation of inequalities both between and within nations. At the heart of this analysis, the interactions with environmental resources entail qualitative transformations of materials and human practices. Of course, by no means all qualitative transformations of environmental resources generate significant amounts of greenhouse gases, some even the reverse. But as so many depend, directly or indirectly, on feeding humans and exploiting fossil energy resources, a major historical leap in the qualitative transformation of environmental resources, such as the British industrial revolution, accelerates climate change with unprecedented rapidity. Forging iron, heating houses, powering steam engines, breeding and rearing sheep and cattle, ploughing up the land, designing and making a combustion engine, designing and driving turbines, turning crude oil into plastic: to list but a few, these qualitative transformations are the food and fuel of climate change.

So, returning to the example of the British development of the cotton textile industry, it encapsulates the connections between qualitative transformations of environmental resources; the co-generation of inequalities; and climate change. As we have seen, there was a radical transformation of the qualities of clothing worn across the world, a range of clothing additional to rather than suppressing wool, linen or leather. Within a few short decades there were new quality distinctions in cotton textiles. Cotton dressed the very slaves that produced the fibre, and was distributed to workhouses under Poor Relief in Britain. At the same time, a rather different quality of cotton fabrics and prints dressed the wealthiest in society, luxury items produced domestically rather than imported as in the early eighteenth century. Cotton textiles became a vehicle of quality distinction, and remain so today. In conjunction with these inequalities of consumption, there was the creation of capital wealth of slaveowners and factory magnates, as against the penury of slaves and the poverty of textile wage workers. New forms of inequality emerged, and continued to change and develop. And all this generated climate change, with the burning of coal in steam-powered cotton mills and the conversion of land into capitalist commercial agriculture by the genocidal replacement of subsistence farmer and hunter-gather Native

Americans. That whole complex web of connections is what the concept of sociogenesis aims to capture.

The two subsequent waves of climate change acceleration highlighted in this book, the electrification and motorisation of society, coincided with the development of universal education systems in nationally very different ways. Qualifications of labour, and different quality of skills and wage systems, contributed to new divisions of labour for different qualitative transformations of objects or actions: carpenters and hair-dressers, coal miners and oil rig workers, web designers and building labourers, farmers and genetic scientists, doctors and refuse collectors, chemical engineers and heavy goods vehicle drivers. Managers and executives obtained positions of power to reward themselves liberally in multinational companies. New hierarchies of income inequalities spread across the world, but with huge differences in the social processes of qualification, labour markets, and enterprise organisation. The stratospheric salaries of celebrities or CEOs are not exceptions to the rule of who gets paid what, but the result of the rule of qualitative exceptionalities. Distinction pays, uniqueness pays better. And neither distinction nor uniqueness are given, but developed, manufactured even, often branded.

The inequalities arising from capital ownership, production systems and labour markets, are then expressed in the consumption of quality distinguished goods, from houses to cars, clothes to food, refrigerators to home entertainment. Distinction is deeply embedded in lifestyles, the whole complex of social practices related to the manifestations of wealth and poverty. As analysed in Chapter 6, the richest within the richest nations consequently manifest these inequalities of wealth in their generation of greenhouse gases by consuming quality distinctions of goods created in production. The top 10% of US consumers generate 50 tonnes of CO_2 equivalent per capita per year, compared to the top 10% of UK consumers at 24 tonnes of CO_2 equivalent per capita, or 14 and 13 tonnes of CO_2 equivalent per capita for Germany and France respectively. That the UK top 10% is responsible for half their counterparts in the USA corresponds to the fact that their incomes are roughly half that of their US counterparts. In spite of a remarkable convergence in wealth, the consumption of the richest 10% of Chinese is equivalent in purchasing power to the bottom 40% decile of American citizens, with a corresponding difference in greenhouse gas emissions. The Top 10 of Americans are in a league of their own whether it comes to cars or household energy, and the average American is in a league of their own for eating meat.

These inequalities or purchasing power within unequal nations, moreover, translate into the key components of climate change. The rich can spread their consumption over a whole paraphernalia of goods and services beyond the basics necessities of social life. Nonetheless, it is remarkable that if the average American burns 4 to 5 times more petrol on than the average Europeans, the top 10% of Americans consume a similar multiple more petrol than the bottom decile of Americans. The Top 10 consumers of petrol and domestic utilities of gas and electricity still account for well over half of their greenhouse gas emissions from all their expenditure on consumer goods. They lead the world in burning up the planet, followed closely on their heels by many not quite so wealthy, and catching-up nations.

From this analysis, it is clear that the societal connections between unequal exploitation of environmental resources, inequalities in wealth, and unequal generation of greenhouse gases are dynamically related to each other. The challenge of the climate emergency is much wider and deeper than the responsibilities of the top 1%, let alone the 1,289 (at the last count) global billionaires. The purchasing power over environmental resources goes all the way up the different income and wealth hierarchies of nations. Systems of quality distinction created in production are tied to patterns of quality distinguished lifestyles of consumption, the very fabric of daily living for the rich, the not so rich, and the bottom 40%, in the different nations of the world.

The societal co-generation of inequalities of wealth and climate change is at the core of what has got us into the climate emergency.

OUT OF THE CLIMATE EMERGENCY ???

Today we use 100 million barrels of oil every day.
There are no politics to change that. There are no
rules to keep that oil in the ground.
So we can't save the world by playing by the rules.
Because the rules have to be changed. Everything has
to change.
And it has to start today.
So everyone out there: it is now time for civil
disobedience.
It is time to rebel.

p. 11
Greta Thunberg, G. 2019. *No one is too small to*
make a difference. Penguin. London.

Under the auspices of the United Nations, the Paris Agreement of 2015 was undoubtedly an historic milestone in achieving commitments to climate change mitigation. Given the decade of tortuous negotiations preceding it, there can be no question that it was a breakthrough at the international and intergovernmental level. At the same time, as the World Scientists' warning letter on the climate emergency demonstrates, the Agreement was deeply flawed in its ambition, its design and its implementation. As already noted, since 2015 greenhouse gas emissions have continued inexorably to rise, and the world is pushing from risk to irreversible change on every significant planetary boundary.

This book has been written in the midst of the COVID-19 pandemic. Many states have reacted to this immediate and life-threatening emergency with unprecedented peace-time economic and political interventions. Some (China, Taiwan, Japan, Germany) have been relatively successful. But overall, there are as many if not more examples of governmental failure. In the two countries to have withdrawn from the Paris Agreement, the USA and Brazil, climate change denial has been matched with Covid-19 denial, in both cases accompanied by a rejection or even repudiation of scientific knowledge. The brutal truth is that political responses to the COVID emergency, whether national or international, cannot inspire confidence in the political institutions necessary to address the much more challenging climate emergency.

In these circumstances, Greta Thunberg is right. Politics as we know it have failed. Initiated by Thunberg's sit-in in front of the Swedish parliament on 9 September 2018, the school strike movement as a form of civil disobedience led by school students rapidly expanded into a global movement. Her speeches to the United Nations and climate conferences (Thunberg, 2019), a high profile journey in a yacht across the Atlantic, placed the climate emergency in the forefront of multiple political arenas. On 15 March 2019, a historically unprecedented school strike by nearly 2 million students spread across more than 120 countries. A more disruptive form of civil disobedience then emerged with the formation and international spread of Extinction Rebellion. Occupations of strategic economic centres in London and other cities had the explicit aims of causing maximum economic impact over extended periods of time, as well as ensuring a high news profile in the media. Many participants had the deliberate aim of being arrested in order to 'occupy' both police and law court time (Extinction Rebellion, 2019).

With demands to accelerate an 80% reduction of greenhouse gas emissions by 2030, both Thunberg and Extinction Rebellion have undoubtedly increased the pressure on national governments to act with greater urgency. They have both embraced the more stringent IPCC target of a 1.5°C limit of global warming. In exerting political pressure on governments by growing movements of civil disobedience, some version of a Green New Deal has been widely supported as the most explicit instrument of change. But in doing so, these movements recognise that national governments are the only game in town capable of bringing about sufficiently radical and rapid decarbonisation transitions. Indeed, whether it is the Green New Deal of the American Sunrise Movement (Prakash & Girgenti, 2020), or the one most widely promoted in the United Kingdom (Green New Deal Group, 2019; Pettifor, 2020), they are explicitly crafted as national solutions for a particular nation state, the USA or the UK. The European Union's policy framework for climate change and energy preceding the Paris Agreement was committed to a 20% cut in greenhouse gas emissions, a 20% share of renewable energy, and a 20% increase in energy efficiency, a policy that has been increasingly exposed for its inadequacy in addressing the climate emergency. The European Commission consequently proposed a much accelerated decarbonisation transition, with a minimum of a 55% reduction in greenhouse gases by 2030, calling the policy the EU Green Deal.

By adopting the language of a New Deal, these various Green New Deals share a vision in which the state and democratic politics play a strategically important role in bringing about a comprehensive transformation of national economies.

More than an intervention to lift the American economy out of the Great Depression, perhaps the most pertinent element of Roosevelt's New Deal of the 1930s was his response to a major, and quintessentially sociogenic, environmental catastrophe, the Dust Bowl. An unfettered market-oriented commercial agriculture destroyed the whole ecosystem of the Southern Plains, leading to massive topsoil erosion and the eventual catastrophe of successive mammoth dust-storms. The farming population, and many small farmers, were left destitute and forced to migrate from their homes, cattle and crops buried under the dust. Roosevelt's New Deal response was both one of environmental restoration and a massive programme of job creation and re-skilling (Worster, 2004). In that case, the sociogenic creation of the catastrophe hit hardest the very people who created it, and within many of their adult lifetimes. It was an immediate emergency with a relatively immediate response.

The current advocates of Green New Deals evoke an impending if not so immediate catastrophe – even the human species extinction. The COVID-19 pandemic and resultant steep economic recessions have prompted a fusion of the immediate economic emergency with the climate emergency as a double imperative for massive state intervention. Some notable economists consider a wartime economy of national existential threat as the appropriate parallel: 'Climate change is our World War III' (Joseph Stiglitz in Prakash & Girgenti, 2020, p. 100). Exceptional circumstances justify exceptional measures. When defending against existential national threat, the level of national debt ceases to inhibit necessary investments.

A common feature of Green New Deals embraces the need for debt-financed infrastructural change, across the economy, for replacement of fossil by renewable energy distributed through smart grids; a restructuring of transport systems using electric or hydrogen cell vehicles; a retro- and re-design of the built environment for energy efficiency; and a sustainable agriculture. Unlike war-debt, however, all the Green New Deal proposals argue that the costs of not investing will eventually hugely outweigh the debts incurred. The havoc brought about by hurricanes and raging fires, or by the flooding of low-lying land as in Bangladesh and the South Pacific islands, are only a foretaste of the scale of economic damage anticipated from global warming above 1.5°C. Thus the UK Green New Deal suggests a £100 billion annual investment over 10 years to bring about the necessary economic transformation, a short-term cost for long-term gain.

Most versions of the Green New Deal involve an extension of public or collective ownership of energy infrastructures, given their diagnosis that the climate emergency is in large part driven by unfettered markets and the power of finance capital. Many suggest that capitalism as we now know it is incompatible with environmental sustainability. But the Green New Deal concept is a recognition of the need to bring about drastic climate change mitigation in the immediate timeframe. As one advocate put it: 'We don't imagine ending capitalism that quickly' (Aronoff et al., 2019, p. 5). This radical socio-economic transformation therefore contains many other dimensions necessary for radical climate change mitigation. All versions insist on a 'just transition', namely that destruction of the old planet-burning economies must be combined with the creation of a new world of employment and skills, and a more equal world. Sustainable agriculture, re-wilding and reforestation address central issues of land use and land use change. Elements of the 'circular economy' are widely shared in the Green New Deal vision, with an insistence on recycling of materials, re-use and repair, an end to the market driven throw-away, planned rapid-obsolescence, economy. Major changes of norms and routines of consumption follow, satisfying finite needs more than infinite manufactured wants. In short, with varied emphasis, they all ask us to imagine a whole different quality of social life.

Green New Deals should not be condemned for Green New Dreaming. We need to dream to escape from the nightmare. But, entering the second decade of the twentieth century, these projects have yet to break through into the centre stage of politics. Following a sit-in of the Sunrise Movement, Congresswoman Alexandria Occasio-Cortez and Senator Ed Markey did place a Green New Deal resolution to Congress. But as yet, it has not been adopted by the Democrats, and as I write, with Trump on his way out, and Biden becoming President, John Kerry will become climate change Tsar, as the erstwhile American signatory of the Paris Agreement. For the foreseeable future, America as the way-out-in-front climate-changing nation, will be mired in Democrat-Republican con-flict paralysis in Congress and the Senate. More fundamen-tally, the old party structures still command the political arena. The absence of green egalitarian parties as the domi-nant parties in new political formations anywhere across the world reflect a political institutional lock-in to a pre-climate change epoch.

Undoubtedly, the various Green New Deals have correctly highlighted the radical pace and scale of change necessary to address the climate emergency and the essential role of dem-ocratic politics and national governments in bringing that change about. They contrast their scope and ambition with the limitations of the Paris Agreement, and the national plans and commitments contained within it. Yet the Green New Deal projects are still to a considerable degree locked-in to a concept of the economy-in-society detached from their resource environments, or those over which nations and cor-porations can command. This has serious consequences. They are conspicuously restricted to advanced industrial nations, and only marginally address the significance of the inequalities between nations for the generation of climate change, let alone within nations.

They evoke self-sufficiency for the Green New Deal economy (e.g. Pettifor, 2020). Yet a self-sufficient economy for the USA or Brazil is quite a different prospect, as we have seen, from self-sufficiency for China with its relative lack of agricultural land and water resources, let alone many other countries of the world. Resource environments are very unequally distributed between countries, including for those elements so critical for a future green economy: fertile land, sun, water, wind, tide. Solar energy is far from equally distributed. Less noticed, China as the world's largest producer and consumer of lithium, has commercially acquired a dominant global position to secure its lithium imports. It produces half from its own environmental resources, and imports half, notably from the largest reserves found in Chile, followed by Argentina. Lithium is not infinite, and not equally distributed, yet it is already a key component of lithium-ion batteries for the green economy of the future. So, the sociogenesis analysis of the climate emergency, with its concept of the socio-economy firmly planted in its resource environment, calls for more.

Once one recognises that the generation of inequalities and the generation of climate change are part of the same process, in various historical trajectories of growth in different nations in their different resource environments, then the political structures of contemporary societies seem obsolete. They were forged in the historical contexts of different battles and conflicts, when social inequalities were treated as a separate and dominant field of contestation. Yet, differences in the wealth of the rich within the rich nations give them purchasing power to unequal claims over the earth's resources. The greater the claims over earth's resources, the greater is the impact of unequal wealth in generating climate change.

The term 'exploitation of nature' can have an almost
neutral ring about it. Humans benefit from nature's 'free gifts',
as discussed in Chapter 2, or 'appropriate Nature's productions in a form adapted to their own demands', as cited at
the head of this chapter. When the term 'exploitation' is
applied to human labour it bears with it the sense of injustice,
whether exploitation is of slavery, indentured labour or wage
labour, whether exploitation is of women's domestic labour
or child labour, or whether exploitation is of migrant or ethnic
minority labour. As my friend the political philosopher,
Norman Geras, wrote, exploitation may denote the economic
process whereby a capitalist appropriates the surplus labour
of the wage worker. But, setting aside Marx's nineteenth
century labour theory of value, it also involves a moral
judgement of the unjust distribution of the wealth created by
human labour in all its varieties and qualities as discussed
above (Geras, 1985; Harvey & Geras, 2018). Whether
through ownership of capital or inheritance, or through the
extreme income hierarchies of large monopoly corporations
and even public organisations, levels of inequality are beyond
legitimacy. The historical emergence of new wealth inequalities examined in this book – through the exploitation of
labour - involve at the same time the unequal appropriation of
unequally distributed environmental resources. The British
colonisation of slave plantations in the Caribbean and Indian
Ocean were the font of its wealth and at the same time a
climate changing exploitation of an acquired resource environment. The settler colonialism of North America was at
once the illegitimate expropriation of Native American land
and a climate changing exploitation of its acquired environmental resource. Exploitation of nature acquires the moral
meaning of an illegitimately unequal command, whether by
force or by economic power, over the earth's environmental
resources. The unjustly unequal command over environmental

resources whether by a richer nation or by the rich within a richer nation, whether of fossil energy resources, land, water or minerals, have been the historical motor of climate change. Exploitation of labour and exploitation of earth's environmental resources are the flipsides of the same coin, and they are at the core of the sociogenesis of climate change.

It may be utopian thinking, but the climate emergency brings into question the very concept of a nation state's absolute rights over its territorial environmental resources, or those it obtains by means of conquest or asymmetric trading power. If a country has coal or oil, it can no longer have a right to burn it. If it has the Amazon forest, then it can no longer have the right to destroy it for national economic gain. A universalisation of environmental regulation for planetary sustainability, covering trade and national territorial exploitation of resources, like human rights legislation, becomes critical for establishing a transnational public goods commons of earth's resources. The accidental geographically unequal distribution of environmental resources cannot legitimate their unequal appropriation, generating illegitimate inequalities of wealth between and within nations. Like the revolutionary and modern legal construct of the 'human' in human rights, a right to a just distribution of the wealth created by labour's qualitative transformations of environmental resources becomes a human right in a shared planet. The urgent measures necessary to address the climate emergency are only the first steps in a long, difficult, even endless, road in which humanity takes collective ownership and responsibility for the sustainability of the planet, in all its biodiversity, its atmosphere, oceans, minerals and chemicals. To bring to an end the socially unjust exploitation of nature.

GLOSSARY

ABCD	Archer Daniels Midland, Bunghe, Cargill and Dreyfus group of global grain traders
CAR	Cadastro Ambiental Rural, Brazilian land registry
CfCs	Chlorofluorocarbons
COP21	Conference of the Parties, number 21, under the UN framework agreement on climate change. Held in Paris in 2015
FAO	Food and Agriculture Organisation of the United Nations
GDP	Gross Domestic Product
GHG	Greenhouse gases
CO_2	Carbon dioxide
CH_4	Methane
NO_x	Nitrous oxide
N_2O	Nitrogen oxide, especially from chemical fertilizer
IBAMA	Institute of Environment and Renewable Resources, Brazil
INPE	Instituto Nacional de Pesquisas Espaciais, National Institute of Space Research, Brazil
IPCC	International Panel on Climate Change
M-C-M^{plus}	Money-Commodities-Money plus (e.g. profit)
MNC	Multinational Corporation
OPEC	Organisation of Petroleum Exporting Countries
PDEC	Production-Distribution-Exchange-Consumption
Ppm	Parts per million
WTO	World Trade Organisation

REFERENCES

ABIEC (Associação Brasiliera dos Indústrias Exportadores de Carne). (2015). Annual statistical report. Retrieved from www.abiec.com.br

ABIEC (Associação Brasiliera dos Indústrias Exportadores de Carne). (2016). *Annual Statistical Report*. Retrieved from www.abiec.com.br

Agrawal, A., Nepstad, D., & Chatre, A. (2011). Reducing emissions from deforestation and forest degradation. *Annual Review of Environment and Resources*, 36, 373–396.

Alencar, A., Nepstad, D., Mendoza, E., Soares-Filho, B., Moutinho, P., Stabile, M. C. C., … Stella, O. (2012). *Acre state's progress towards jurisdictional REDD+*. Brasília, DF: Instituto de Pesquisa Ambiental da Amazônia. 53p.

Allen, R. C. (2009). *The British industrial revolution in global perspective*. Cambridge: Cambridge University Press.

Altvater, E. (2016). The capitalocene, or, geoengineering against capitalism's planetary boundaries. In J. W. Moore (Ed.), *Anthropocene or capitalocene* (pp. 138–152). Oakland, CA: PM Press.

Anderson, G. C. (2019). *The conquest of Texas: Ethnic cleansing in the promised land, 1820–1875*. Norman, OK: University of Oklahoma Press.

Aronoff, K., Battistoni, A., Cohen, D. A., & Riofrancos, T. (2019). *A planet to win: Why we need a green new deal.* London: Verso Books.

Bai, J., Wahl, T. I., Lohmar, B. T., & Huang, J. (2010). Food away from home in Beijing: Effects of wealth, time and "free" meals. *China Economic Review, 21*(3), 432–441.

Beckert, S. (2015). *Empire of cotton: A global history.* New York, NY: Vintage.

Bishko, C. J. (1952). The peninsular background of Latin American cattle ranching. *The Hispanic American Historical Review, 32*(4), 491–515.

Bowes, J. P. (2014). American Indian Removal beyond the Removal Act. *Journal of the Native American and Indigenous Studies Association, 1*(1), 65–87.

Bowling, G. A. (1942). The introduction of cattle into colonial North America. *Journal of Dairy Science, 25*(2), 129–154.

Brown-Lima, C., Cooney, M., & Cleary, D. (2010). An overview of the Brazil-China soybean trade and its strategic implications for conservation. The Nature Conservancy, Brazil.

Cardoso, A. S., Berndt, A., Leytem, A., Alves, B. J., de Carvalho, I. D. N., de Barros Soares, L. H., … Boddey, R. M. (2016). Impact of the intensification of beef production in Brazil on greenhouse gas emissions and land use. *Agricultural Systems, 143*, 86–96.

Carlson, L. A., & Roberts, M. A. (2006). Indian lands,"Squatterism," and slavery: Economic interests and the passage of the Indian removal act of 1830. *Explorations in Economic History, 43*(3), 486–504.

Carvalho de Rezende, D., & Alberto Rodrigues Silva, M. (2013). Eating-out and experiential consumption: A typology of experience providers. *British Food Journal, 116*(1), 91–103.

Cerri, C. C., Moreira, C. S., Alves, P. A., Raucci, G. S., de Almeida Castigioni, B., Mello, F. F., ... Cerri, C. E. P. (2016). Assessing the carbon footprint of beef cattle in Brazil: A case study with 22 farms in the State of Mato Grossosss. *Journal of Cleaner Production, 112*, 2593–2600.

Chancel, L., & Piketty, T. (2015). Carbon and inequality: From Kyoto to Paris Trends in the global inequality of carbon emissions (1998–2013) & prospects for an equitable adaptation fund. *World Inequality Laboratory*. Retrieved from https://halshs.archives-ouvertes.fr/halshs-02655266/document

Clark, B., & Foster, J. B. (2009). Ecological imperialism and the global metabolic rift: Unequal exchange and the guano/nitrates trade. *International Journal of Comparative Sociology, 50*(3–4), 311–334.

Cohn, A. S., Mosnier, A., Havlík, P., Valin, H., Herrero, M., Schmid, E., ... Obersteiner, M. (2014). Cattle ranching intensification in Brazil can reduce global greenhouse gas emissions by sparing land from deforestation. *Proceedings of the National Academy of Sciences, 111*(20), 7236–7241.

Coopersmith, J. (2016). *The electrification of Russia, 1880–1926.* Ithaca, NY: Cornell University Press.

Correa, P., & Schmidt, C. (2014). Public research organizations and agricultural development in Brazil: How did Embrapa get it right? *Economic Premise, 145*, 1–10.

Cronon, W. (1991). *Nature's metropolis: Chicago and the Great West.* New York, NY: WW Norton & Company.

Crutzen, P. J. (2002). Geology of mankind. *Nature*, *415*, 23.

Crutzen, P. J., & Stoermer, E. F. (2000). The "anthropocene". *Global Change Newsletter*, *41*, 17–18.

Druckman, A., & Jackson, T. (2009). The carbon footprint of UK households 1990–2004: A socio-economically disaggregated, quasi-multi-regional input–output model. *Ecological Economics*, *68*(7), 2066–2077.

EIA (US Energy Information Agency). (2019). Retrieved from https://www.eia.gov/international/data/world

EIA (US Energy Information Agency). (2020). Monthly report. Retrieved from https://www.eia.gov/outlooks/ieo/pdf/transportation.pdf

Escobar, H. (2019). Brazilian president attacks deforestation data. *Science*, *365*(6452), 419.

Evans, P. (1979). *Dependent development: The alliance of multinational, national and local capital in Brazil*. Princeton, NJ: Princeton University Press.

Evans, R. J. (1990). *Death in Hamburg: Society and politics in the cholera years, 1830–1910*. London: Penguin.

Extinction Rebellion. (2019). *This is not a drill. An Extinction rebellion handbook*. London: Penguin.

FAO. (2013a). *Guidelines to control water pollution from agriculture in China*. Rome.

FAO. (2013b). *Tackling climate change through livestock. A global assessment of emissions and mitigation opportunities*. Rome.

Fearnside, P. M. (2001). Soybean cultivation as a threat to the environment in Brazil. *Environmental Conservation*, *28*(1), 23–38.

Fearnside, P. M. (2005). Deforestation in Brazilian Amazonia: History, rates, and consequences. *Conservation Biology*, *19*(3), 680–688.

Fearnside, P. M. (2008). The roles and movements of actors in the deforestation of Brazilian Amazonia. *Ecology and Society*, *13*(1), 23.

Fearnside, P. M., & Figueiredo, A. M. (2015). China's influence on deforestation in Brazilian Amazonia: A growing force in the state of Mato Grosso. BU Global Economic Governance Initiative Discussion Chapters, 3.

Fearnside, P. M., Figueiredo, A. M., & Bonjour, S. C. (2013). Amazonian forest loss and the long reach of China's influence. *Environment, Development and Sustainability*, *15*(2), 325–338.

Ficek, R. E. (2019). Cattle, capital, colonization: Tracking creatures of the Anthropocene in and out of human projects. *Current Anthropology*, *60*(S20), S260–S271.

Flink, J. J. (1970). *America adopts the automobile, 1895-1910* (p. 55). Cambridge, MA: MIT Press.

Flink, J. J. (1988). *The automobile age*. Cambridge, MA: MIT Press.

Foster, J. B. (2000). *Marx's ecology: Materialism and nature*. New York, NY: Monthly Review Press.

Foster, J. B. (2013). Marx and the rift in the universal metabolism of nature. *Monthly Review*, *65*(7), 1–20.

Fuller, D. Q. (2010). An emerging paradigm shift in the origins of agriculture. *General Anthropology*, *17*(2), 1–12.

Fuller, D. Q., Van Etten, J., Manning, K., Castillo, C., Kingwell-Banham, E., Weisskopf, A., … Hijmans, R. J. (2011). The contribution of rice agriculture and livestock pastoralism to prehistoric methane levels: An archaeological assessment. *The Holocene, 21*(5), 743–759.

Gale, H. F., Hansen, J., & Jewison, M. (2015). China's growing demand for agricultural imports. USDA-ERS Economic Information Bulletin 136.

Gale, F., Valdes, C., & Ash, M. (2019). *Interdependence of China, United States, and Brazil in Soybean Trade* (pp. 1–48). New York, NY: US Department of Agriculture's Economic Research Service (ERS) Report.

Galenson, D. (1974). The end of the Chisholm Trail. *The Journal of Economic History, 34*(2), 350–364.

Gard, W. (1953). The Shawnee Trail. *The Southwestern Historical Quarterly, 56*(3), 359–377.

Gard, W. (1967). The impact of the cattle trails. *The Southwestern Historical Quarterly, 71*(1), 1–6.

Garnett, T., & Wilkes, A. (2014). Appetite for change. Social, economic and environmental transformations in China's food system. *Food Climate Research Network*. Retrieved from www.fcrn.org.uk

Garrett, R. D., Lambin, E. F., & Naylor, R. L. (2013). Land institutions and supply chain configurations as determinants of soybean planted area and yields in Brazil. *Land Use Policy, 31*, 385–396.

Geras, N. (1985). The controversy about Marx and justice. *New Left Review, 150*(3), 47–85.

Gibbs, H. K., Munger, J., L'Roe, J., Barreto, P., Pereira, R., Christie, M., … Walker, N. F. (2016). Did ranchers and slaughterhouses respond to zero-deforestation agreements in the Brazilian Amazon? *Conservation Letters, 9*(1), 32–42.

Gill, M., Feliciano, D., Macdiarmid, J., & Smith, P. (2015). The environmental impact of nutrition transition in three case study countries. *Food Security, 7*(3), 493–504.

Glucksmann, M. (1990). *Women assemble: Women workers and the new industries in inter-war Britain*. London: Routledge.

Green New Deal Group. (2019). The Green New Deal. A bill to make it happen. Retrieved from https://greennewdealgroup.org/wp-content/uploads/2019/09/GND_A_Bill_To_Make_It_Happen.pdf

Hall, A. L. (2008). Better RED than dead: Paying the people for environmental services in Amazonia. *Philosophical Transactions of the Royal Society B: Biological Sciences, 363*, 1925–1932.

Hansen, J., & Gale, F. (2014). China in the next decade: Rising meat demand and growing imports of feed. *Amber Waves*. Retrieved from http://www.ers.usda.gov/amber-waves/2014-april/china-in-the-next-decade-rising-meat-demand-and-growing-imports-of-feed.aspx#.V71ukaLKZc4

Harley, C. K. (2004). Trade: Discovery, mercantilism and technology. *The Cambridge Economic History of Modern Britain, 1*, 1700–1860. 175–203.

Harvey, M. (2007). Instituting economic processes in society. In *Karl Polanyi: New perspectives on the place of the economy in society* (pp. 163–184). Manchester: Manchester University Press.

Harvey, M. (2014). The food-energy-climate change trilemma: Toward a socio-economic analysis. *Theory, Culture & Society, 31*(5), 155–182.

Harvey, M. (2015). *Drinking water: A socio-economic analysis of historical and societal change 2015*. London: Routledge.

Harvey, M. (2019, October). Slavery, indenture and the development of British industrial capitalism. *History Workshop Journal, 88,* 66–88.

Harvey, M., & Bharucha, Z. P. (2016). Political orientations, state regulation and biofuels in the context of the food–energy–climate change trilemma. In *Global bioethanol* (pp. 63–92). London: Academic Press; Elsevier.

Harvey, M., & Geras, N. (2018). *Inequality and democratic egalitarianism: 'Marx's economy and beyond' and other essays.* Manchester: Manchester University Press.

Harvey, M., & Pilgrim, S. (2011). The new competition for land: Food, energy, and climate change. *Food Policy, 36,* S40–S51.

Harvey, M., & McMeekin, A. (2005). Brazilian genomics and bioinformatics: Instituting new innovation pathways in a global context. *Economy and Society, 34*(4), 634–658.

Hecht, S. B. (1993). The logic of livestock and deforestation in Amazonia. *Bioscience, 43*(10), 687–695.

Hecht, S. B. (2012). From eco-catastrophe to zero deforestation? Interdisciplinarities, politics, environmentalisms and reduced clearing in Amazonia. *Environmental Conservation, 39*(1), 4–19.

Hopewell, K. (2014). The transformation of state-business relations in an emerging economy: The case of Brazilian agribusiness. *Critical Perspectives on International Business, 10*(4), 291–309.

Hopewell, K. (2016). The accidental agro-power: Constructing comparative advantage in Brazil. *New Political Economy, 21,* 536–554.

Hornborg, A. (2012). *Global ecology and unequal exchange: Fetishism in a zero-sum world* (Vol. 13). London: Routledge.

Hornborg, A. (2014). Ecological economics, Marxism, and technological progress: Some explorations of the conceptual foundations of theories of ecologically unequal exchange. *Ecological Economics, 105*, 11–18.

Hornborg, A. (2016). Post-capitalist ecologies: Energy, "value" and fetishism in the Anthropocene. *Capitalism Nature Socialism, 27*(4), 61–76.

Hornborg, A. (2019). The money–energy–technology complex and ecological marxism: Rethinking the concept of "use-value" to extend our understanding of unequal exchange, part 2. *Capitalism Nature Socialism, 30*(4), 71–86.

Huang, J., & Rozelle, S. (2009). *Agricultural development and nutrition: The policies behind China's success*. Beijing: World Food Programme.

Hudson, P. (2002). *The genesis of industrial capital: A study of West Riding wool textile industry, c. 1750–1850*. Cambridge: Cambridge University Press.

Hudson, P. (2008). The limits of wool and the potential of cotton in the eighteenth and early nineteenth centuries. In G. Riello & P. Parthasarathi (Eds.), *The spinning world* (pp. 327–350). Oxford: Oxford University Press.

Hughes, T. P. (1983). *Networks of power: Electrification in Western society, 1880–1930*. Baltimore, MD: Johns Hopkins University Press.

IEA. (2019). Growing preference for SUVs challenges emissions reductions in passenger car market. Paris: IEA. Retrieved from https://www.iea.org/commentaries/growing-preference-for-suvs-challenges-emissions-reductions-in-passenger-car-market

IEA. (2020). Global Energy Review 2020. The impacts of the Covid 19 crisis on global energy demand and CO_2 emissions. Retrieved from www.iea.org

IEA (International Energy Authority). (2018). The future of cooling: Opportunities for energy-efficient air conditioning. Retrieved from www.iea.org

IPCC. (2018). *An IPCC special report on the impacts of global warming of 1.5°C*. Retrieved from https://www.ipcc.ch/sr15/

IPCC. (2019). *Climate change and land*. Retrieved from https://www.ipcc.ch/srccl/

Jepson, W., Brannstrom, C., & Filippi, A. (2010). Access regimes and regional land change in the Brazilian Cerrado, 1972–2002. *Annals of the Association of American Geographers, 100*(1), 87–111.

Koopman, R. B., & Laney, K. (2012). *Brazil: Competitive factors in Brazil affecting US and Brazilian agricultural sales in selected third country markets* (p. 4310). US International Trade Commission Publication.

Latawiec, A. E., Strassburg, B. B. N., Valentim, J. F., Ramos, F., & Alves-Pinto, H. N. (2014). Intensification of cattle ranching production systems: Socioeconomic and environmental synergies and risks in Brazil. *Animal, 8*(8), 1255–1263.

Lewis, T. (1997). *Divided highways: Building the interstate highways, transforming American life*. New York, NY: Penguin.

Lichtenberg, E., & Ding, C. (2008). Assessing farmland protection policy in China. *Land Use Policy, 25*(1), 59–68.

Liu, X., Vitousek, P., Chang, Y., Zhang, W., Matson, P., & Zhang, F. (2015). Evidence for a historic change occurring in China. *Environmental Science & Technology*, *50*(2), 505–506.

Liu, X., Zhang, Y., Han, W., Tang, A., Shen, J., Cui, Z., ... Fangmeier, A. (2013). Enhanced nitrogen deposition over China. *Nature*, *494*(7438), 459–462.

Love, C. M. (1916). History of the cattle industry in the Southwest, II. *The Southwestern Historical Quarterly*, *20*(1), 1–18.

Lu, Y., Jenkins, A., Ferrier, R. C., Bailey, M., Gordon, I. J., Song, S., ... Feng, Z. (2015). Addressing China's grand challenge of achieving food security while ensuring environmental sustainability. *Science Advances*, *1*(1), p. e1400039.

Ma, H., Huang, J., Fuller, F., & Rozelle, S. (2006). Getting rich and eating out: Consumption of food away from home in urban China. *Canadian Journal of Agricultural Economics/Revue canadienne d'agroeconomie*, *54*(1), 101–119.

Macedo, M. N., DeFries, R. S., Morton, D. C., Stickler, C. M., Galford, G. L., & Shimabukuro, Y. E. (2012). Decoupling of deforestation and soy production in the southern Amazon during the late 2000s. *Proceedings of the National Academy of Sciences*, *109*(4), 1341–1346.

Malanima, P. (2006). Energy crisis and growth 1650–1850: The European deviation in a comparative perspective. *Journal of Global History*, *1*(1), 101–121.

Malm, A. (2016). *Fossil capital: The rise of steam power and the roots of global warming*. London: Verso Books.

Martha, G. B., Alves, E., & Contini, E. (2012a). Land-saving approaches and beef production growth in Brazil. *Agricultural Systems, 110,* 173–177.

Martha, G. B., Contini, E., & Alves, E. (2012b). Embrapa: Its origins and changes. In W. Beir (Ed.), *The regional impact of national policies: The case of Brazil* (pp. 204–226). Cheltenham: Edward Elgar.

McCraw, T. K. (1976). Triumph and irony—The TVA. *Proceedings of the IEEE, 64*(9), 1372–1380.

McGlade, C., & Ekins, P. (2015). The geographical distribution of fossil fuels unused when limiting global warming to 2 C. *Nature, 517*(7533), 187–190.

McNichol, D. (2006). *The roads that built America. The incredible story of the US Interstate System.* New York, NY: Sterling Press.

Melillo, E. D. (2012). The first green revolution: Debt peonage and the making of the nitrogen fertilizer trade, 1840–1930. *The American Historical Review, 117*(4), 1028–1060.

Meyer, W. B., & Turner, B. L. (1992). Human population growth and global land-use/cover change. *Annual Review of Ecology and Systematics, 23*(1), 39–61.

Mier y Terán Giménez Cacho, M. (2016). Soybean agri-food systems dynamics and the diversity of farming styles on the agricultural frontier in Mato Grosso, Brazil. *The Journal of Peasant Studies, 43*(2), 419–441.

Minchinton, W. (1990). The rise and fall of the British coal industry: A review article. *VSWG: Vierteljahrschrift für Sozial-und Wirtschaftsgeschichte, 77*(H. 2), 212–226.

Mintz, S. W. (1986). *Sweetness and power: The place of sugar in modern history.* London: Penguin.

Mitchell, T. (2011). *Carbon democracy: Political power in the age of oil*. London: Verso Books.

Mokyr, J., Sarid, A., & van der Beek, K. (2019, November 7). *The wheels of change: Human capital, millwrights, and industrialization in eighteenth-century England*. London: Centre for Economic Policy Research.

Moore, J. W. (2009). Madeira, sugar, and the conquest of nature in the "first" sixteenth century: Part I: From "Island of timber" to sugar revolution, 1420–1506. *Review (Fernand Braudel Center)*, 345–390.

Moore, J. W. (2010). Madeira, sugar, and the conquest of nature in the "first" sixteenth century, part II: From regional crisis to commodity frontier, 1506—1530. *Review (Fernand Braudel Center)*, 1–24.

Moore, J. W. (2014). The end of cheap nature, or, how I learned to stop worrying about'the'environment and love the crisis of capitalism. In *Structures of the world political economy and the future of global conflict and cooperation* (pp. 285–314). Wien: LIT Verlag.

Moore, J. W. (2015). *Capitalism in the web of life: Ecology and the accumulation of capital*. London: Verso Books.

Moore, J. W. (2017). The capitalocene, part I: On the nature and origins of our ecological crisis. *The Journal of Peasant Studies*, *44*(3), 594–630.

Moore, J. W. (2018). The capitalocene part II: Accumulation by appropriation and the centrality of unpaid work/energy. *The Journal of Peasant Studies*, *45*(2), 237–279.

Mu, Z., Bu, S., & Xue, B. (2014). Environmental legislation in China: Achievements, challenges and trends. *Sustainability*, *6*(12), 8967–8979.

Nepstad, D., McGrath, D., Stickler, C., Alencar, A., Azevedo, A., Swette, B., … Armijo, E. (2014). Slowing Amazon deforestation through public policy and interventions in beef and soy supply chains. *Science, 344*(6188), 1118–1123.

Nepstad, D. C., Stickler, C. M., & Almeida, O. T. (2006). Globalization of the Amazon soy and beef industries: Opportunities for conservation. *Conservation Biology, 20*(6), 1595–1603.

Newell, P., & Taylor, O. (2020). Fiddling while the planet burns? COP25 in perspective. *Globalizations, 17,* 580–592.

Norse, D., & Ju, X. (2015). Environmental costs of China's food security. *Agriculture, Ecosystems & Environment, 209,* 5–14.

Norse, D., Lu, Y., & Huang, J. (2014). China's food security: Is it a national, regional or global issue? In K. Brown (Ed.), *China and the EU in context* (pp. 251–302). Basingstoke: Palgrave Macmillan.

Oliveira, G. D. L. (2016). The geopolitics of Brazilian soybeans. *The Journal of Peasant Studies, 43*(2), 348–372.

de Oliveira Silva, R., Barioni, L. G., Hall, J. A. J., Matsuura, M. F., Albertini, T. Z., Fernandes, F. A., & Moran, D. (2016). Increasing beef production could lower greenhouse gas emissions in Brazil if decoupled from deforestation. *Nature Climate Change, 6,* 493–498.

Oliveira, G. D. L., & Schneider, M. (2016). The politics of flexing soybeans: China, Brazil and global agroindustrial restructuring. *The Journal of Peasant Studies, 43*(1), 167–194.

Oswald, Y., Owen, A., & Steinberger, J. K. (2020). Large inequality in international and intranational energy footprints between income groups and across consumption categories. *Nature Energy, 5*(3), 231–239.

Oxfam International. (2015). Extreme carbon inequality. Retrieved from https://www-cdn.oxfam.org/s3fs-public/file_attachments/mb-extreme-carbon-inequality-021215-en.pdf

Pacheco, P., & Poccard-Chapuis, R. (2012). The complex evolution of cattle ranching development amid market integration and policy shifts in the Brazilian Amazon. *Annals of the Association of American Geographers*, *102*(6), 1366–1390.

Parker, G. (2013). *Global crisis: War, climate change and catastrophe in the seventeenth century*. New Haven, CT: Yale University Press.

Peine, E. K. (2013). Trading on Pork and Beans: Agribusiness and the construction of the Brazil-China-soy-pork commodity complex. In H. S. James (Ed.), *The ethics and economics of agrifood competition* (pp. 193–210). Dordrecht: Springer.

Pereira, E. J. D. A. L., de Santana Ribeiro, L. C., da Silva Freitas, L. F., & de Barros Pereira, H. B. (2020). Brazilian policy and agribusiness damage the Amazon rainforest. *Land Use Policy*, *92*, 104491.

Pereira, P. A. A., Martha, G. B., Santana, C. A., & Alves, E. (2012). The development of Brazilian agriculture: Future technological challenges and opportunities. *Agriculture & Food Security*, *1*(1), 1.

Pereira, R., Simmons, C. S., & Walker, R. (2016). Smallholders, agrarian reform, and globalization in the Brazilian Amazon: Cattle versus the environment. *Land*, *5*(3), 24.

Pettifor, A. (2020). *The case for the green new deal*. London: Verso.

Piketty, T. (2014). *Capital in the twenty-first century*. Cambridge, MA: Harvard University Press.

van der Ploeg, J. D., & Ye, J. (Eds.). (2016). *China's peasant agriculture and rural society: Changing paradigms of farming.* London: Routledge.

Prakash, V., & Girgenti, G. (2020). *Winning the green new deal. Why we must, how we can.* New York, NY: Simon & Schuster.

Ribeiro, C. D. S. G., & Corcao, M. (2013). The consumption of meat in Brazil: Between socio-cultural and nutritional values/O consumo de carne no Brasil: Entre valores socioculturais e nutricionais. *Demetra: Food, Nutrition & Health, 8*(3), 425–452.

Ripple, W. J., Wolf, C., Newsome, T. M., Barnard, P., & Moomaw, W. R. (2019). World scientists' warning of a climate emergency. *BioScience, 70*(1), 8–12.

Ripple, W. J., Wolf, C., Newsome, T. M., Galetti, M., Alamgir, M., Crist, E., … 15,364 scientist signatories from 184 countries (2018). World scientists' warning to humanity: A second notice. *BioScience, 67*(12), 1026–1028.

Rockström, J., Steffen, W., Noone, K., Persson, Å., Chapin, F. S. III, Lambin, E., … Foley, J. (2009). Planetary boundaries: Exploring the safe operating space for humanity. *Ecology and Society, 14*(2), 1–33.

Ruddiman, W. F. (2003). The anthropogenic greenhouse era began thousands of years ago. *Climatic Change, 61*(3), 261–293.

Ruddiman, W. F. (2010). *Plows, plagues, and petroleum: How humans took control of climate* (Vol. 46). Princeton, NJ: Princeton University Press.

Ruddiman, W. F. (2013). The anthropocene. *Annual Review of Earth and Planetary Sciences, 41*, 45–68.

Schneider, M. (2011). Feeding China's pigs: Implications for the environment, China's smallholder farmers and food security. Institute for Agriculture and Trade Policy. Retrieved from http://www.iatp.org/documents/china

Schneider, M. (2016). Dragon head enterprises and the state of agribusiness in China. *Journal of Agrarian Change*, *17*(1), 3–21.

Schneider, M., & Sharma, S. (2014). China's pork miracle? Agribusiness and development in China's pork industry. Institute for Agriculture and Trade Policy. Retrieved from http://www.iatp.org/documents/china

Shand, J. D. (1984). The Reichsautobahn: Symbol for the third Reich. *Journal of Contemporary History*, *19*(2), 189–200.

Sharma, S. (2014). The Need for feed. Institute for Agriculture and Trade Policy. Retrieved from www.iatp.org

Sigsworth, E. M. (1952). The west riding wool textile industry and the great exhibition. *Bulletin of Economic Research*, *4*(1), 21–31.

Smil, V. (2004). *Enriching the earth: Fritz Haber, Carl Bosch, and the transformation of world food production*. Cambridge, MA: MIT Press.

Soler, L. S., Verburg, P. H., & Alves, D. S. (2014). Evolution of land use in the Brazilian Amazon: From frontier expansion to market chain dynamics. *Land*, *3*(3), 981–1014.

Steffen, W., Richardson, K., Rockström, J., Cornell, S. E., Fetzer, I., Bennett, E. M., … Folke, C. (2015). Planetary boundaries: Guiding human development on a changing planet. *Science*, *347*(6223), 1259855.

Steffen, W., Rockström, J., Richardson, K., Lenton, T. M., Folke, C., Liverman, D., ... Donges, J. F. (2018). Trajectories of the Earth System in the Anthropocene. *Proceedings of the National Academy of Sciences*, *115*(33), 8252–8259.

Strassburg, B. B., Latawiec, A. E., Barioni, L. G., Nobre, C. A., da Silva, V. P., Valentim, J. F., ... Assad, E. D. (2014). When enough should be enough: Improving the use of current agricultural lands could meet production demands and spare natural habitats in Brazil. *Global Environmental Change*, *28*, 84–97.

Strokal, M., Ma, L., Bai, Z., Luan, S., Kroeze, C., Oenema, O., ... Zhang, F. (2016). Alarming nutrient pollution of Chinese rivers as a result of agricultural transitions. *Environmental Research Letters*, *11*(2), 024014.

Surdam, D. G. (1997). The Antebellum Texas Cattle Trade across the Gulf of Mexico. *The Southwestern Historical Quarterly*, *100*(4), 477–492.

Thunberg, G. (2019). *No one is too small to make a difference*. London: Penguin.

Tilman, D., Socolow, R., Foley, J. A., Hill, J., Larson, E., Lynd, L., ... Williams, R. (2009). Beneficial biofuels—The food, energy, and environment trilemma. *Science*, *325*(5938), 270–271.

Tooze, A. (2007). *The wages of destruction: The making and breaking of the Nazi economy*. London: Penguin.

Turner, M. (1998). Counting sheep: Waking up to new estimates of livestock numbers in England c 1800. *The Agricultural History Review*, *46*(2), 142–161.

Ummel, K. (2014). Who pollutes? A household-level database of America's greenhouse gas footprint. Center for Global Development Working Paper 381. Retrieved from http://indiaenvironmentportal.org.in/files/file/who-pollutes-database-greenhouse-gas-footprint.pdf

UNDP (2012). The emissions gap report. A UNEP synthesis report. Retrieved from http://www.unep.org/pdf/2012gapreport.pdf

Unruh, G. C. (2000). Understanding carbon lock-in. *Energy Policy*, 28(12), 817–830.

USDA. (2016). Economic research service. Retrieved from http://www.ers.usda.gov/topics/international-markets-trade/countries-regions/brazil/basic-information/Downloaded 08.11.2016

Waldron, S., Brown, C., & Longworth, J. (2010). A critique of high-value supply chains as a means of modernising agriculture in China: The case of the beef industry. *Food Policy*, 35(5), 479–487.

Waldron, S., Jimin, W., Huijie, Z., Xiaoxia, D., & Mingli, W. (2015). The Chinese beef cattle industry. Retrieved from https://www.uq.edu.au/agriculture/docs/CAEG/China.pdf

Wang, J., Chen, Y., Shao, X., Zhang, Y., & Cao, Y. (2012). Land-use changes and policy dimension driving forces in China: Present, trend and future. *Land Use Policy*, 29(4), 737–749.

Wang, J., Huang, J., & Rozelle, S. (2010). Climate change and China's agricultural sector: An overview of impacts, adaptation and mitigation. ICTDS Issue Brief No 5.

Wiedenhofer, D., Guan, D., Liu, Z., Meng, J., Zhang, N., & Wei, Y. M. (2017). Unequal household carbon footprints in China. *Nature Climate Change*, 7(1), 75–80.

Wilkinson, J. (2009). The globalization of agribusiness and developing world food systems. *Monthly Review*, *61*(4), 38.

Wilkinson, J., & Wesz Junior, V. J. (2013). Underlying issues in the emergence of China and Brazil as major global players in the new South–South trade and investment axis. *International Journal of Technology Management & Sustainable Development*, *12*(3), 245–260.

Wootton, H. J. (2004). Traffic forecasting and the appraisal of road schemes. In *The motorway achievement: Volume 1: The British motorway system: Visualisation, policy and administration* (pp. 265–303). London: Thomas Telford.

World Bank. (2014a). World development indicators. Retrieved from http://wdi.worldbank.org

World Bank. (2014b). Changing food consumption patterns in China: Implications for domestic supply and international trade. *The Chinese Economy*. Update 2014. Retrieved from www.worldbank.org/china

Worster, D. (2004). *Dust bowl: The southern plains in the 1930s*. Oxford: Oxford University Press.

Wrigley, E. A. (2000). The divergence of England: The growth of the English economy in the seventeenth and eighteenth centuries: The Prothero Lecture. *Transactions of the Royal Historical Society*, *10*, 117–141.

Wrigley, E. A. (2013). Energy and the English industrial revolution. *Philosophical Transactions of the Royal Society A: Mathematical, Physical and Engineering Sciences*, *371*, 1–10. 20110568.

Ye, J. (2015). Land transfer and the pursuit of agricultural modernization in China. *Journal of Agrarian Change*, *15*(3), 314–337.

Ye, J., Wang, C., Wu, H., He, C., & Liu, J. (2013). Internal migration and left-behind populations in China. *The Journal of Peasant Studies*, 40(6), 1119–1146.

Zhang, F., Chen, X., & Vitousek, P. (2013). Chinese agriculture: An experiment for the world. *Nature*, 497(7447), 33–35.

Zhang, Q. F., & Donaldson, J. A. (2008). The rise of agrarian capitalism with Chinese characteristics: Agricultural modernization, agribusiness and collective land rights. *The China Journal*, 60, 25–47.

Zhang, X., Yin, S., Li, Y., Zhuang, H., Li, C., & Liu, C. (2014). Comparison of greenhouse gas emissions from rice paddy fields under different nitrogen fertilization loads in Chongming Island, Eastern China. *Science of the Total Environment*, 472, 381–388.

Zuo, Q., Jin, R., Ma, J., & Cui, G. (2014). China pursues a strict water resources management system. *Environmental Earth Sciences*, 72(6), 2219–2222.

INDEX